NADI Market Week
June 1980
New York City

DISPLAY
FUNDAMENTALS

display
FUNDAMENTALS
A BASIC DISPLAY MANUAL

Third Edition
Third Printing, 1979

by

FRANK A. ROWE

Published by

SIGNS OF THE TIMES PUBLISHING COMPANY

Cincinnati, Ohio, U.S.A.

THE KEY MAGAZINE/TEXT SYSTEM

Each chapter of this text has been supplemented with a numbering system to identify the subject matter to instructors for educational teaching purposes. The Key Magazine/Text System is designed to assist educators in employing this book as an instructional guide and/or as a classroom text with young persons seeking display knowledge.

This same numerical coding is used in *Visual Merchandising* magazine to identify feature articles that contain additional and current information applicable to the educational process. In this manner, the monthly industry magazine, which covers retail merchandising, point-of-purchase display, exhibitry, museum presentation and store planning on an international scope, offers an up-to-date extension of the fundamentals of display that are presented within the pages of this book.

The numerical key to subject matter is listed here for your reference:

1—Composition
2—Lighting
3—Color
4—Signing
5—Motion
6—Ideas
7—Organization/Management
8—Workshop
9—Installation
10—Budget
11—Tools
12—Props
13—Materials
14—Mannequins
15—Store Planning
16—Shopping Centers/Malls
17—Point-of-Purchase
18—Exhibits
19—Showrooms
20—Museums
21—Special Promotions

foreword

The field of retail merchandising continues to expand at a very rapid rate. In addition to the large chain operations, thousands of small retail stores and specialty shops are operated by independent merchants throughout the nation.

Most independent retail stores do not have specially trained display personnel available to arrange their merchandise in a highly professional manner. It is usually necessary for the owner or manager to perform this function.

This manual is designed to provide, with a minimum of research and study, the basic techniques needed to display merchandise effectively. It will also be of decided value to instructors of merchandising subjects in colleges and evening schools.

The manner in which the basic principles and techniques are presented, with "how-to-do-its" logically and clearly illustrated, should be particularly useful to instructors in retailing, advertising, marketing, and small business management.

Hal C. Cheney
Coordinator of Business Education
Diablo Valley College
Concord, California

TO LEE PILKINGTON,
THE DISPLAYMAN'S DISPLAYMAN

table of contents

preface

A SK THE next display man or woman you meet how he (or she) got into his chosen work. You will probably find it was a rather haphazard thing. In many cases he will have been an art student, more concerned with the development of modern schools of painting than with the application of art in the business world. Only a small percentage of those who embark on a fine arts career succeed in earning a living. Certainly a large number of these drift into display work.

If our hypothetical displayman is not a frustrated Matisse it is likely that he worked in another department, usually sales, within the retail establishment. Perhaps after working with more or less satisfaction as a sales person, he was given additional responsibilities for the attractive presentation of merchandise in his department. Sales persons do far more display work than even they realize. If one thinks of display and merchandise presentation as synonymous terms this fact will become evident. After all, any neat, orderly arrangement of stock *is* display in its most elementary and perhaps most important form.

The next step in the career of our displayman is to request a transfer to the display department, where he can work in the field he enjoys most on a full-time basis.

In either case, of the art student or the sales person, the typical display worker did not choose a display career early in his development and prepare for it in a systematic way, as a person preparing for one of the professions might, or even as skilled craftsmen serve an apprenticeship before becoming journeymen.

Many stores have apprenticeships in their display departments and some are undoubtedly very worth-while training. At best, however, the apprenticeship programs vary widely in quality so that an employer in San Francisco, for example, could not know, without practical tests, if a person who claims to have served an apprenticeship in another part of the country, is really qualified or not.

How often display directors have heard young persons in their departments ask "Where can I find a manual covering the everyday techniques used in my work?" Unfortunately, very little literature on this subject exists. There are books in the libraries with photographs of windows in New York, Paris, and other fashion capitols. But the books that cover the basic techniques in the assembly of a display, books that are valuable to small stores in average American shopping centers where the owner is also the displayman, as well as to young men and women just starting a display career, are badly out of date.

The reasons for writing this manual then, are first, to contribute to the standardization of display training, and second, to phrase it in a way that will be valuable to the widest possible group. It is hoped that not just "soft lines" or "fashion" stores will be able to use it. Hardware stores, paint shops, book stores, antique shops, pet shops, auto parts stores, in fact, every conceivable retail store should be able to find something useful in its pages.

The professional displayman won't find more than a re-statement of his present knowledge. The ultra-artistic trimmers will probably find it too dogmatic. It is not designed primarily for display manufacturers, mannequin manufacturers, sign painters, neon workers, set designers, or all others who can be called display workers in the broadest sense of the term (although it is hoped that they will find some things to interest them). But if it does help a few beginners over the rough spots, so that they can approach display problems with confidence instead of bluffing through, it will have served its purpose.

chapter 1

the revolution in retailing

RETAIL display follows the broader sociological, economic, and technological changes in American life. It has been suggested that the reverse is true, that sales promotion manipulates our taste and desire for consumer goods so as to effect basic changes in our lives. In general, most persons will agree that display mirrors rather than molds.

What are some of the recent changes that have affected display? The most important are:

1. the automobile as our primary means of transportation.
2. the growth of the suburbs.
3. introduction of self-service or automation in retailing.

SHOPPING CENTERS VS. DOWNTOWN STORES

The phenomenal growth of the automobile as our chief means of transportation has had an effect on retailing which, in turn, has affected display. People commute great distances to work in downtown areas. This has stimulated the growth of shopping centers adjacent to suburban residences. Modern shopping center store design channels customer traffic directly to the sales area, with a greatly reduced number of appeals, in the form of windows and exterior displays, between the point where the shopper parks her car and the point where the sale is completed. This means that displaymen working in suburban shopping centers must pay more attention to point-of-purchase displays, the so-called first line of sales promotion. In considering window and exterior displays they must develop ideas that can be seen at a glance. In fact, window and exterior displays for shopping centers facing streets or highways should be keyed to the fleeting vision of a person in a moving automobile.

The changed conditions imposed by the rapid development of suburban shopping centers and the subsequent emphasis on the point-of-sale is making the term "window trimmer" obsolete. The modern displayman must be a triple-threater. He must be able to trim windows, handle any display assignment inside the store, and he must be a capable member of the store's promotional planning team. Only the largest department stores, with display staffs of ten or more persons, can still afford the specialized position of window trimmer. The titles most commonly used today are display director, display manager, or sales promotion director.

A FEW CHARACTERISTICS OF DOWNTOWN STORES AND SHOPPING CENTERS

Shopping Centers	*Downtown Stores*
1. Store can be designed laterally. The only impediment to expansion is the sacrifice of parking space.	1. Building is vertical. Expansion also must be vertical.
2. Shoppers dress is more permissive. Younger families, more emphasis on children's needs and sportswear.	2. Older, more diverse background. Shoppers feel more obliged to dress.
3. Almost unlimited parking.	3. Limited parking.
4. Heavy automobile traffic.	4. More foot traffic because of the location of parking.
5. Fewer display windows.	5. More emphasis on display windows.

Of course, this summary does not pretend to exhaust the differences between downtown stores and shopping centers. It only suggests a few that are most applicable to the display job.

A comparison of the two major retail areas is in some ways an exposure of their weaknesses and strengths. For example, most downtown stores have more square feet devoted to display windows. This creates

Fig. 1. The architect's drawing, above, enables the owner to visualize how the new front would appear. A comparison of this sketch with a photograph of the completed store would indicate how factual a perspective drawing can be.

Fig. 2. Mall entrance to Halle Bros., Severence Shopping Center, Cleveland, Ohio.

Fig. 3 and Fig. 4. The author's concept of how the typical, cluttered Main Street (below) could be changed into a model shopping mall, as indicated above.

traffic in the store but it also means a large overhead in the larger display staff that must be retained to maintain both windows and point-of-purchase displays.

Similarly, it was thought that the permissive characteristics of the suburban centers (slacks and shorts, hair in rollers, etc.) stimulated larger numbers of persons to shop. To a certain extent this is true. On the other hand, wise merchants and their display managers are learning that the dressed-up feel of the downtown areas is one of the intangible pleasures of shopping to many women. In every case, the displayman's job of creating a store image can do a lot to control the shopping tastes of the customers. If the store looks like a rummage sale, the ladies will wear slacks, downtown or in the suburbs. If it looks like Saks, they'll tend to dress accordingly. This matter of image is something the store management must consciously determine and work to create.

While the huge parking lot is undoubtedly a tremendous advantage to the suburban center, there is no denying that many of them are greater eyesores than concealed rooftop or underground parking areas being developed by progressive "downtown" merchants.

So, any comparison of downtown and suburban shopping centers can be a two-edged sword. Every display manager should, with the rest of the store planning team, analyze his situation (start by listing the advantages and disadvantages much as we have done here). What appeared to be a disadvantage can often be turned to an advantage by an alert, imaginative display *manager*.

Of course, he can't run out and build an underground parking lot, if this seems to be indicated, but he might, for example, discover that a window on a side street has very little "pull." It might be wise, then, to recommend that this window be trimmed once every two weeks instead of each week, thereby releasing the display staff for more important tasks. This is the kind of suggestion that is within the range of practical application every day. The bigger things, like the underground parking lot, don't have to be forgotten, but can be developed on a long-term basis. The real point of all this is to show that displaymen are not passive recipients of orders from store management. They are imaginative, creative members of the management staff.

AUTOMATED SELLING

The invention of electronic computers, the utilization of advanced methods of communication and transportation, and modern, scientific store and fixture design, has brought about an ever-increasing amount of automation in retailing. In retail terms it is called "self-service" or "self-selection." It does not take as many people to bring the finished product from the factory to the consumer. In several chains, for example, inventory and ordering of most staple merchandise is done by computers in a central office from stubs torn from sales slips.

Some displaymen have watched these developments with alarm. With the elimination of whole job classifications, they saw their position in the retail structure endangered. Actually, these fears are poorly founded. Rather than a smaller role, displaymen can expect a larger and more important role in the future.

Self-service does not mean no service. The person who used to point out the selling points of the merchandise is being replaced by "silent salesmen," that is, by signs, and by display of the merchandise in a way to create a desire to buy. From the viewpoint of the displaced salesperson, it is an unfortunate fact that the displayman is the substitute for personal contact that permits reduction of the store staff.

Naturally, there are some lines that will always require the attentions of a live salesperson. But it is also very erroneous to think that shoppers like to be waited on for every purchase. Much of the fun of shopping is the chance to inspect and turn the merchandise, to read the descriptions and study the labels, all without the constant hovering about of an eager sales person who is obviously more concerned about a difficult sales quota than real service.

The efficient and profitable presentation of merchandise for this kind of self-service is the great challenge that faces displaymen today. Those who recognize the challenge will find the future replete with opportunities rather than diminishing prospects of employment.

STORE HOURS

The trend in retail establishments is toward more open nights. More and more persons find it inconvenient to shop during the weekday hours. The very competitive retail industry has responded by staying open more nights. Managers in some suburban centers estimate that as much as 75% of their total volume comes on open nights and Saturdays. The practice varies from one to seven nights a week, depending on the competition, the character of the store, etc.

What does this mean for displaymen? Simply that the displayman, instead of being in the store at the hours of peak volume, should attempt to regulate his hours to be finished when customer traffic is heaviest and to work when there is the least traffic.

It is not only hard to get things done when shoppers block the aisles but it is more dangerous for everyone and certainly annoying to the shopper to be pushed and shoved by mannequin carts, rolls of seamless paper, and other equipment of the displayman.

Fig. 5 and 6: Above is typical window display of John Wanamaker, Philadelphia department store in 1925; below is a modern window treatment with highly stylized mannequins.

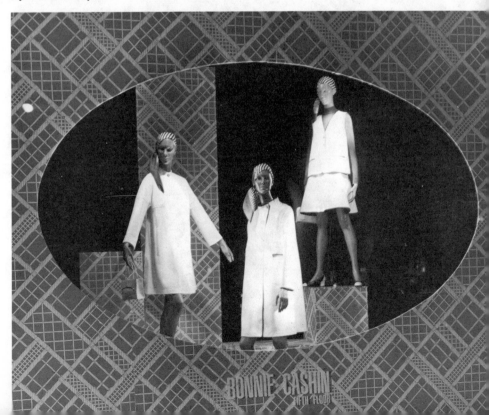

Fig. 7

Fig. 8

At one time much of the trimming was done at night and in the early morning hours when the store was closed (in some stores this is still true). The advantages of this system are obvious. It's easier for the display staff to work, the customers are never confronted with torn-up displays, it is safer for everyone involved, and the displays can be "pulled" and replaced more efficiently and quickly.

The main drawbacks to night and early morning hours are equally obvious. In small departments the display manager must attend to administrative duties, sit in on planning meetings, etc. All this is in addition to installing the displays. This would mean a 24-hour day. Experienced displaymen will smile when they read this and say "That's what I've been doing for years." But sooner or later, something has to give; either the administration of the department will suffer, the trims will look rushed, or the displayman himself will conk out.

In some cases, night work is prohibitive because of premium wage rates required by union contracts. In each case the display manager must weigh the circumstances that apply to his store and choose the hours that are the best all around for the job, for customer convenience, for living within the budget, and for his personal needs.

Another aspect of display hours contrasted with the sales staff, is that a winter vacation is sometimes better than summer. Most stores set-up holiday trims about November 1. Once the holiday trim is set (about November 15 in most cases), it is possible to let some display people take time off. Since Christmas is the "heaviest" trim of the year, there is less basic changing to be done. Many stores leave the same window backgrounds and interior displays for almost two months, although this would seem to be too long. Conversely, some stores have two complete Christmas window trims. While sales-people are as busy as can be, displaymen, particularly interior display personnel, find they are less rushed than they will be immediately after Christmas and at other seasons of the year.

BASIC IDEAS IN THE MIDST OF CHANGE

We are amused when we look at an old display manual because the styles are so out of date. Two things will never become out of date, however. The first is *neatness* in every action of the displayman. The second is the limitation imposed on his design by the architecture of the store. The last point is called the *Frame of Reference* for the purposes of this manual.

NEATNESS

While fixtures, store design, and concepts of retailing change, neatness will remain a constant in display work. Indeed, the word trim is almost synonymous with neat. Nothing can spoil an otherwise good trim faster than a carelessly left thread, a pin on the floor, dust on the mannequin bases or on the window moldings, or any other evidence of dirt. Remember that most shoppers are housewives who take pride in cleanliness!

The habit of neatness in display is easy to develop. If a few elementary rules are established, the rule will soon become a habit. Sample rules are:

1. to always wear window socks or to remove shoes before entering carpeted display areas.

2. to always dust mannequin bases as the last step in every trim.

3. to always check finished windows from outside for loose threads, dirt, etc.

The biggest single step towards effective displays will have been taken when such rules are enforced.

Here are a few little tricks for keeping displays neat and clean:

1. Add a tiny amount of ammonia to water for cleaning any glass or plastic.

2. A tiny amount of vinegar in water makes a good (and less expensive) mannequin cleaner. Know if your mannequins are plastic or papier mache and plaster before using water, however. Dampness can penetrate the lacquer and plaster skin of some mannequins, causing permanent damage. Modern plastic mannequins, on the other hand, can be submerged in water without harm. Vinegar in water will also bring paint brushes clean as new.

3. Roll up a ball of masking tape (adhesive out) for a very good eraser. It is better for removing lint from garments than any commercial preparation. Of course, it isn't a replacement for a whisk broom, but it is very helpful where a whisk broom might disturb delicate draping.

4. Change lights that are burned out *before* instead of *after* installation of a display. Much dirt and dust is inevitably dislodged in this operation.

5. Keep your tools in a box, an apron, a belt holder, or some other appropriate place instead of scattering them all over the display area. Too often, things are forgotten at clean-up time.

FRAMES OF REFERENCE

No one knows better than a painter how important the four sides of the picture are to his composition. Instead of taking them for granted, they are the starting point for everything in the picture.

The displayman also learns to pay close attention to the basic framework of his composition. In display work it is harder to recognize than in painting. Instead of a two-dimensional plane, the displayman works with depth. The front edges of a window become mixed with the side walls, and in interior displays the whole composition is backed by planes running to many perspective points. In short, everything in the display is competing with the store architecture. The skilled displayman learns to make the architecture work for him. He also unitizes his displays by actually using or at least thinking in terms of frames.

As a general rule, where natural edges do not exist, such as the walls of a window, it is advisable to create a limit or frame of some sort. In this way attention is directed to the important elements of the display. The viewer's eye is held on the display rather than being distracted by the store architecture.

The *Frame of Reference* may be a store window. It may be a screen behind a mannequin. It might be a real picture frame used in the display of jewelry and other small items. Some stores have been very successful with inexpensive frames used over and over as the basic framework of all displays. The open space in the frame is filled with wood lattice, wire screen, yarn, or any of many materials to suspend the merchandise.

The displayman who arranges merchandise for presentation on a TV screen must think in terms of an imaginary frame. The TV screen in your home is a real enough frame, but the displayman doesn't see it except remotely. In spite of his difficulty in seeing his *Frame of Reference* he must consider it in order to create a good display.

To sum up, one can say that the basic display task, in terms of composition, is to arrange the elements of the display in an appealing and tasteful way within a real or imaginary frame.

chapter 2

where displaymen work

BECAUSE store categories are constantly changing, it might be well to list a few of the places where displaymen will be found.

2

9

15

1. *Department Stores:* As the name implies, the store is divided into departments. Within this category there are many variations. Some feature soft lines, some have limited self-service while others build their reputation on personal service. This type of store, with specialty shops, has been the traditional employer of display specialists.

2. *Supermarkets and Drug Centers:* Supermarkets are basically large, modern grocery stores. Many "supers" have so-called drug stores under the same roof. This type of store evolved from a prescription drug store, and still retains this department, although it is sometimes hard to find. The "drug stores" carry everything from auto parts to dog food. Supermarkets are now rapidly expanding in the areas of soft-goods and housewares.

Displaymen, when they are employed by this type of store, often double as sign painters or ad layout artists. Display consists of massive "end" displays. This is primarily a matter of orderly arrangement and is usually the job of clerks rather than display specialists.

3. *Discount Stores:* A comparative newcomer to the retail field, discount stores carry much the same merchandise as department stores, differing chiefly in their emphasis on low overhead and self-service. In actual practice, discount stores are up-grading their displays while some department stores are borrowing the best characteristics of the discounter. This may result in the eventual replacement of both with something incorporating the best features of both. The conditions listed with reference to the employment of display specialists in supermarkets would also apply to discount stores. While discounters do not do a lot of trimming, in the traditional sense of that term, there is a big opportunity for displaymen interested in fixtures and store design.

4. *Specialty Shops:* Ladies ready-to-wear, men's wear, children's or infants' wear, or any other shop featuring limited lines can be called a specialty shop. This is the province of many free-lance displaymen. The specialty shop, without the budget for a full-time display staff, either trains clerks for display work or calls in a free-lancer who may service several shops.

5. *Variety Stores:* Originally planned to sell merchandise within a limited, low price range, variety stores are in the process of merchandise and price upgrading so that an inter-mingling of categories has resulted. The term "junior department store" has been coined to describe the more progressive variety stores. This category usually trains a girl to do display work, make signs, and sell part-time.

HOW WE SEE DISPLAYS

It is very important to station one's self in front of a store window or interior display and observe customer reaction. Nothing is more informative. How we see displays is more complex than we thought.

First, count the persons who pass the window or display in a ten-minute period. Then, in a second ten-minute period, count those who actually stop. They will be a fairly small percentage. But this does not mean that those who don't stop did not see it. In some cases it is possible to go one step further and count those who purchase the item after studying the display.

In seeing displays it is a matter of concentration that distinguishes one shopper from another. While a few really study, the majority only see in passing. Their eyes are arrested only by the most attention compelling displays. These facts are ripe with implication for the imaginative displayman.

ANALYSIS OF THE STORE

A general couldn't hope to win a battle without a knowledge of the topography. Neither can a displayman hope to do a good job unless he knows his store. As a first step, he should obtain a blueprint showing the location of tables and all key display areas. If the original blueprint is not available or is not up to date, he can devise his own chart. Exact scale is not as important as the location of display areas and the direction and amount of customer traffic.

As soon as he has marked the most important facts about customer traffic on his chart and has numbered all display areas, the displayman is in a better position to recommend displays that will sell. He is able to plan more efficiently.

It may be a good idea to break down the numbering on the chart. One set of numbers might be for tables on peak traffic aisles. Another would be for stock-keeping tables or gondolas. Another set might be for perimeters and ledges, another for show cases, and perhaps still another for booths. In larger stores it may be best to break it down by floors or departments. The exact system is not important. It must be practical for your situation.

Many displaymen go one step further and actually mark all tables. This can be done with small pieces of masking tape placed out of sight in a uniform location. The department manager, as well as the displayman, can then use the table number in discussing or requisitioning displays.

The display chart will become one of the displayman's most valuable tools. It is a good idea to mount it in the display office. Use an acetate overlay and crayon to indicate the current promotions.

Some displaymen are very analytical. They can, for example, say that for a given number of people passing a display, an approximate number will stop to study. Of those that stop to study, a predictable number will make a purchase. Of course, this does not take into account the large number who know what they want and shop accordingly. It is a means of gauging "impulse" or "related item" sales.

What are the commonly accepted terms that a displayman will want to use on his chart? Let us list the terms, first with reference to windows, and second, with reference to interior displays.

TYPES OF WINDOWS

Store architecture creates many variations, but windows are basically one of four types. These (as the diagram shows) are *straight*, *"L" corner*, and *island*. Each shape has its advantages and disadvantages. For example, the *straight* window is the easiest to trim. The commercial jingle "It's what's up front that counts" is certainly apropos in window trimming. It's all right to use all the pins, wire, tape, and other devices you please to hold the thing together so long as none of it shows from the front. The other kinds of windows, while more difficult, offer opportunities for original and dramatic effects that the straight window does not.

Modern shopping centers utilize open-back windows to a large extent. In this type of construction the shopper looks into the store and can often see every corner of the interior at a glance. Window displays are either not used at all or are installed in one of several ways.

If the entire store is the only display nothing more is done than to see that the glass is clean. Washing the glass, by the way, is one of the most important steps in trimming a window, and one of the most neglected. In larger stores the actual washing is done by the custodial staff, but the display department has the responsibility for seeing that it is done properly and regularly.

A low railing or ornamental grille is sometimes used at the back of an open-back window. An easily removed screen makes a more complete background. Probably the most effective displays are those that cause the store interior to work as part of the design. In other words, instead of fighting the problem, the displayman makes it work for him.

INTERIOR DISPLAY AREAS

The many kinds of display areas in retail stores are not very well standardized. In many cases they are not even well thought out for the job they must do. Fortunate indeed is the displayman who is consulted by architects before the store is built.

He could tell the architect that different kinds of merchandise are shown to the best advantage in settings planned for their embellishment. Furniture window and interior displays, for example, should be near to or on the floor or street level to obtain the effect of a real room. The windows of a clothing store should be from twelve to twenty-four inches higher than the sidewalk. Of course, probably the most common oversight is the location of the display workshop and display storage areas. As a result, countless hours are lost in needless movement from the shop to the display areas.

One hears words like *end, island, box,* and *cap* in talking with displaymen. The following definitions will illustrate a few of the interior display areas that are generally recognized.

1. *Cap or End:* These refer to tables located on peak traffic aisles. *End* is used by supermarkets and discount stores. *Cap* is usually used by department stores and specialty shops. The back-up stock can be on the same table or on adjacent tables.

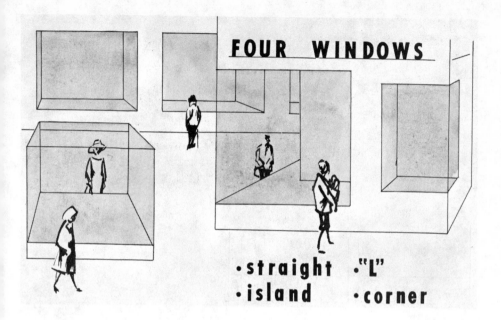

FOUR WINDOWS

- straight • "L"
- island • corner

Fig. 9

Fig. 10

WOMENS SPORTSWE

Fig. 11 Fig. 12

2. *Islands:* This display area gets its name from the fact that it is surrounded by a "sea" of customer traffic. Stock-keeping tables are not necessarily nearby. A similar display area used in supermarkets and discount stores is called a *dump* display because the merchandise is thrown into the container in a haphazard way. The container is often related to the merchandise. For example, a small boat for water skis, a shopping cart for canned goods, or a trailer for camping gear. If the merchandise is not stocked at the *island* area it is important that a sign gives clear directions. An *island* window has the same characteristics as an interior display area except that it is enclosed by glass.

3. *Perimeters:* What was considered waste space in many stores can be put to profitable use by an ingenious person. Sometimes perimeter displays consist of panels, constructed of perforated hardboard, cork or similar wallboards. In other cases they consist of displays built along the ledges. In general, perimeter displays are used to establish an over-all promotional idea, to identify a season, or to introduce a department. Cap tables, rather than perimeters, are used to promote specific items.

4. *Box:* A small window or display case usually used to spotlight specific items. Jewelry, cosmetics, handbags, hosiery, or other small items are displayed in boxes.

5. *Booths or Bays:* Many stores find this display area very profitable. Stock tables are arranged around a rectangle or square with the sales person and cash register in the center. Booths are good for "hot" sale items, clearance events, and specials. Usually they are decorated with an overhead canopy plus a sign to identify the merchandise.

6. *Showcase:* A fixture that encloses the merchandise so that it is visible to the customer but out of reach. It is valuable to department stores and specialty shops for the prestige it lends to the merchandise. It is also useful in discount stores, variety stores, and the like to protect small articles that are prone to pilferage.

7. *Open Display Tables or Gondolas:* These are the basic stock keeping tables in modern stores. The most modern examples provide for a maximum of self-service and flexibility. They should be designed so that the shelves can be removed and replaced easily, to accommodate various merchandise.

8. *Counter Tops:* Counter tops are utilized as display areas. Three-quarter length mannequins are designed for use with them. Another variation is a glass or metal shelf on the racks used in dress shops. The chief consideration in preparing displays for these

areas is the avoidance of a cluttered, over-trimmed look, and customer utility. If the particular top adorns a self-service unit, the display must not interfere in any way.

9. *Platform Displays:* These are similar to a *cap* or *end* table in function and similar to an *island* display in construction. They are usually placed at the ends of aisles. Each consists of a low platform, perhaps a mannequin dressed in the merchandise being sold on adjacent racks, a background screen, and a sign.

10. *Column Displays:* Lots of displaymen consider the columns the big guns of their display arsenal. As a matter of fact, the strictly utilitarian function of a store column is to support the roof. In the most modern buildings, lightweight metals and advanced technology permit the elimination of many columns. Where they remain, it is best to use them for over-all seasonal atmosphere, departmental identification, and price event posters. Most stores put up their heaviest column displays in the holiday season.

Many of these words will come up again when we get into the subject of store planning and fixturing in Chapter 10.

WINDOW CONSTRUCTION

Possibly the most troublesome problem in window construction is the elimination of reflections. The basic problem is simply that the sun, being more intense than the window lights, will cause the window glass to act as a mirror. Thus, the shops across the street and passing cars may become more visible than the merchandise. In this hemisphere, of course, the best situated stores, as regards reflections, are those that face north. Those that face east are subjected to intense morning sunlight, while those that face west are subjected to the afternoon rays. Several suggestions can be made to control the inter-related problem of reflections and window heat.

In the first place, some stores with a little foresight have the window glass installed at a slight angle, with the top of the glass further from the building than the bottom, so the sun rays are not reflected directly into the customers' eyes. Building costs are slightly higher, but this also eliminates a problem that would persist through the life of the building.

Awnings are used to control reflection as well as to protect customers from the elements and to reduce window heat. The chief objection most displaymen have to awnings is the dilapidated condition of many of them and the reluctance of management to spend the money to maintain them properly. All of us have seen otherwise attractive stores disgraced by dirty, torn, floppy awnings.

Fig. 13

Fig. 15

Of course, modern canvas awnings, or the light-weight metal variety, can enhance a building, if they are properly maintained. Even with the best awnings there must be a system for putting them up and down or else they will be up when they should be down and vice versa.

Short of basic architecture or permanent or temporary awnings, the following suggestions will help control window glare:

1. Use light colored window backgrounds. This brings the light in the window into closer balance with the sun's rays. The specific color choice will depend on other factors. If the window walls cannot be painted frequently, a natural beige or grey is probably best. Three or four changes annually to suggest the seasons is not unreasonable with modern latex base paints. Contrast with the value and hue of the merchandise is necessary. Thus the color choice for the wall must be weighed carefully, balancing the factors of window reflection, merchandise contrast, and promotional appeal.

2. Leave the window lights on during daylight hours. The extra cost will be offset by increased customer traffic.

3. Where contrast cannot be achieved between merchandise and the window wall, use flats covered with paint, paper, or cloth behind merchandise to achieve contrast.

4. Backlighting in the window will not eliminate reflections in itself, but has the same effect as a colored background in achieving contrast.

5. Plastic coatings for window glass are available to minimize reflections. In one installation, it is applied to the interior of the glass in liquid form. The manufacturer claims reflections are substantially reduced, window temperature lowered, the plastic coating is invisible, and damage to merchandise from fading is greatly reduced.

In another form, plastic sheets can be lowered inside the glass during the hottest part of the day. This method will prevent fading but it is not used except in extreme conditions because the amber or green color distorts the display.

The professional way to trim is to cover the inside of the window glass with a curtain or screen while the work is in progress. This is neater, especially if trimming is done during shopping hours. It also stimulates the curiosity of passersby. Curiosity can be stimulated even more by using messages on the screen such as "Watch This Window for Another Outstanding Value," etc.

Many materials are available for window construction. The following paragraphs will give some idea of the good and bad points of some of the most widely used.

1. *Floor Coverings:* Heavy duty carpeting in a neutral shade is possibly the most popular. Seasonal colors can be added with grass

mats, scatter grass, wood chips, shredded paper, shredded plastic, etc.

Architects too often overlook the necessity for pinning to the floor in almost every window change. If the carpet has been put down over a concrete slab, the displayman must either install a wooden sub-floor himself or devise a window fixture for pinning.

A heavy duty carpet permits unlimited pinning through to the wooden sub-floor without marks. In selecting carpet, it is wise to choose one with a slight texture or tweed effect as this will not show dirt as readily as a solid color. Competent companies can shampoo a good window carpet after several years, bringing it back to almost new appearance.

Similar to carpet, in many respects, is the system of fabric covered wallboard for a floor covering. The usual practice is to cut four to eight sections of wallboard, depending on the window size. They are numbered on the back for ease of assembly and storage. Notches must be cut to accommodate columns and other permanent obstructions.

Wallboard floor panels have the very desirable characteristic of easy pinning without showing marks. Color selection is more versatile than with the permanent carpet floor covering, although it will be necessary to always wear window socks on the more delicate fabrics. The use of panels has two real disadvantages. It can be quite expensive to cover floor panels several times a year. Also, many displaymen find that they don't have time to pull the panels out of the window, re-cover them, and then install the new display. If either of these conditions apply, a permanent carpet may be the answer.

Good fabrics for covering panels are denim, sailcloth, osnaburg, indian head, monk's cloth, and burlap. In certain trims the rather costly use of velveteen or satin may be justified.

Vinyl floors are sometimes used for windows. They are easy to clean. They have the big drawback that every experienced displayman will point out, namely that it is impossible to pin to them without marks showing. Moreover, their effect is somewhat cold and lacking in richness. Vinyl floors are used quite often in appliance stores, hardware stores, and other stores featuring hard lines. The best application of vinyl is to lay the square in place over a good, flat sub-floor; in this way pinning can be accomplished between the squares.

Flagstone, terra-cotta, natural brick, or painted brick make modern display floors. Here again, they should be used with merchandise that does not require attachment to the floor. Like the vinyl floor tiles this handicap is overcome if time permits their temporary use rather than permanent installation.

2. *Dividers and Ceiling Grids:* These have been placed under the same heading because they should be designed as a single unit. The

best divider designs are removable, permitting many variations of the window dimensions. This means that they are usually suspended from the ceiling grid.

In some cases, flats with clamp-on legs are used as dividers but they will not stand vertically as easily as a divider that hangs.

An effective ceiling grid can be constructed with 1 x 2 inch lumber. A heavy-weight wire or metal tube can be used to construct a ceiling grid or it is possible to purchase grids from fixture manufacturers to order for any ceiling size. Ceiling grids are not always used in small shop windows, particularly those with low ceilings. In larger stores, and those with high ceilings, frequent change schedules, and heavy merchandise, a good grid is a necessity. The time necessary to install a grid is far less than that to tack and nail to the ceiling every time the window is changed.

The best material for window dividers is that which is lightest yet rigid enough not to warp under high window temperatures. Aluminum is a good all-round material for this purpose.

3. *Lights:* Good display lighting can do more than any other ingredient, yet it is the most neglected by the displayman. Many otherwise excellent entries in display contests have been disqualified because of bad lighting.

Sometimes the displayman wants to *wash* the display with light. In others he wants to *spotlight* parts of the display. In most instances, he will use a combination of the two techniques. *Washing* and *spotlighting* then are the basis for most display lighting. Specific lamps have been designed for each function.

Spotlights are always of the incandescent variety. Lights to *wash* the display can be incandescent or fluorescent. By contrast with fluorescent's cool light, incandescent lights have a slightly yellowish character.

In general, incandescent spotlights are high wattage bulbs known as "Par" (or parabolic) or lower wattage bulbs (around 150 watts) with clear glass and a reflector mounted in the back of the bulb and known as "R" (for reflector). The choice in this case is difficult.

From the cost standpoint, "Par" bulbs have a higher initial cost but will last from 2000 to 3000 hours. The 150 watt "R" type bulb has a low initial cost but burns out faster. In fairness to both, it must be stated that cost tests have been inconclusive.

Floodlights, or lights to *wash* the display, are, as has been mentioned, either fluorescent or incandescent but with frosted glass. In every case, the best lamps are manufactured to transmit heat to the rear. This helps to prolong the life of delicate props and prevents damage to merchandise.

An effective and increasingly popular practice is back-lighting. Back-lights are usually fluorescent tubes concealed on the floor at the back of the window. The box that conceals the tubes is usually covered with the same material as the floor covering. Fluorescent tubes are available in either white or colors. The whites have several subdivisions; each with its own color characteristics. The dealer can recommend the best for color definition. This gives the displayman an extremely versatile tool for *washing* the display with light to (a) contrast with the merchandise, (b) set a seasonal character to the display, (c) to unify the composition, (d) to stop the eyes of passersby.

Important factors in determining the number of light fixtures for a window are distance and over-loading. The distance from the merchandise is very important because lights lose their foot-candle power surprisingly fast as they are moved away from an object. Of course, overloading circuits must also be considered carefully in determining the number of fixtures. The best advice is to consult an electrician, but a quick rule for safety is to multiply amperage (usually indicated by a number on the fuse, 15A, 20A, 30A, etc.) by the line voltage (usually 120 volts but always available from your utility company). This figure will be the number of watts that can be used safely on one circuit. For example, if a 15 amp fuse is used and the line voltage is 120, then 1800 watts can be used on the circuit with safety.

In addition to the basic incandescent or fluorescent lights for spotlighting or washing the display, a wide number of specialty lights are available. These include rotating colors, twinkle lights, flashers, etc. These have their place as eye-catchers but cannot replace the basic light plan.

Several basic principles for the employment of light should be considered by the apprentice displayman. The word "considered" is used advisedly because there are no hard and fast rules about display lighting. These are, however, things that many displaymen have found worked for them.

a. Display lights are generally most effective when they are crossed. The furthest left light in the bank is directed to the far right corner, the furthest right is directed to the left corner, and so on. Crossing lights results in a more even, diffused light, without the disconcerting "roller-coaster" effect of bright and dim areas caused by lights directed straight ahead.

b. Save white lights for the merchandise. The shopper should see the merchandise as perfect as possible, without a wrinkle or loose thread. But it should not be distorted in any way. This would result if colored light was used excessively. Colored lights should be played

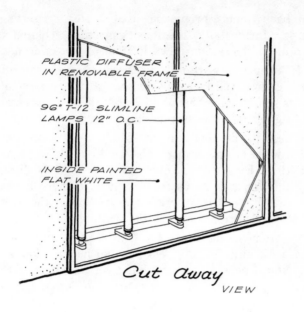

PLASTIC DIFFUSER
IN REMOVABLE FRAME

96" T-12 SLIMLINE
LAMPS 12" O.C.

INSIDE PAINTED
FLAT WHITE

Cut away VIEW

Fig. 16

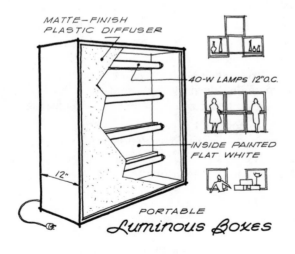

MATTE-FINISH
PLASTIC DIFFUSER

40-W LAMPS 12" O.C.

INSIDE PAINTED
FLAT WHITE

12"

PORTABLE
Luminous Boxes

on the backgrounds, props, and used to create a setting for the merchandise. Incidentally, the most convenient colored lights are the clip-on filters that are installed in front of white incandescent bulbs.

c. If mannequins are used in the display, be careful not to direct spots at elbows, full-face, at the shoes, at the wig, or in any way that distracts from the merchandise by making the light on an unimportant thing brighter than the surrounding light.

d. Check the lighting at night. Many a displayman has been rudely shocked when he saw at night the window that looked so beautiful in the daytime. Every tiny wrinkle will show up in the display illuminated only with electric light. Of course, this is as much if not more a problem of pressing. At least, a night inspection of the window will show what has to be pressed over in the morning.

e. Diagram the light plan for each display until experience permits you to work intuitively. Check the finished window against the diagram. You may find that you didn't get the effect you planned.

f. Replace burned out bulbs with each change. If this isn't done, the store is apt to be dark and apparently closed at a very embarrasing moment, like a busy open night. Store managers take a very dim view of replacing lights themselves at such times.

g. Have a policy for turning lights on and off. Most modern stores have time clocks that can be set for turn on and off hours.

h. Never place hot electrical fixtures close to inflammable objects. Some communities have ordinances covering this. Eighteen inches is an approximate minimum. Always check closely before leaving the display area to ascertain that light fixtures cannot fall, drift in their swivels, or become dislodged by the vibration of a passing vehicle. If there is any question about safety, remove the doubtful fixture!

i. Find ways to conceal light cords. Sometimes they can run under rugs. Sometimes they can be concealed behind props. If they have to be exposed, run them as straight as possible parallel to and up against the molding at the back of the display.

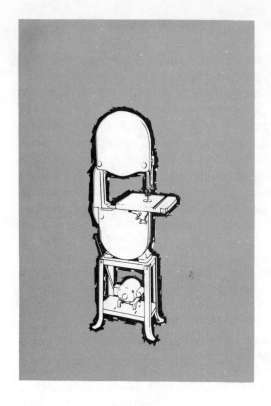

chapter 3

the display shop

DISPLAY work isn't different from other human endeavor in that order and planning are essential. This is obscured sometimes by the popular misconception that displaymen are temperamental geniuses who thrive in the midst of chaos. While it may be true that there are such displaymen, it is also true that the consistently good jobs are done by persons with a well developed sense of order.

The first step in establishing order in the display department is a clean, well lighted and ventilated workshop. What functions are performed in the display shop?

1. Merchandise presentation plans are developed.
2. Display props are built, converted for seasonal changes, and adapted to convey sales messages.
3. Forms and mannequins are dressed for use throughout the store.
4. Display fixtures and props are painted.

5. Signs are prepared, either with a machine, hand lettered, or with cut-out letters.

6. Fixtures, props, mannequins, tools, small hardware, etc., used by the entire store (not just the display staff) are stored.

This list will give a fair idea of the way space in the display shop should be allocated. The following paragraphs will outline basic considerations in shop planning as it relates to each of these functions:

1. An office is necessary for developing plans. If this seems to belabor the obvious, it should be stated that too many displaymen try to work without one. In addition to planning, the office is used for interviews with salesmen, for records of the success or failure of promotions, and in small stores, a desk for the preparation of ad layouts is sometimes installed in the display office. Minimum furniture should be a desk and typewriter, a fixture chart (this was described in Chapter 2), a file cabinet, and a sales promotion calendar. A convenient device is to rule off a 4 by 8-foot sheet of painted hardboard for a three-month period or season. Important change dates, promotions, etc., are recorded with crayon on an acetate cover. The whole thing can be erased at the end of each three-month period.

2. A large work table is necessary for building props. Its size, and the size of adjacent storage areas for seamless paper, wallboard, cloth, etc., will depend on how much building is actually done. This varies considerably. Chain department stores, for example, do very little building. Their props are lithographed or silk screen printed posters shipped from a central warehouse plus foliage and set pieces purchased from a display manufacturer. They are usually purchased at a discount because orders are placed for the entire chain. This does not mean that the chain store will do no building, but it does indicate that the space necessary for this function will not be as much as that for an independent store.

3. A storage area for display forms and mannequins must be included in the shop plan. Supplementary mannequin storage adjacent to the windows so that window mannequins can be stored with minimal movement is desirable if the display shop is not near the windows.

The mannequin "bin" must be clean and well lighted. A system must be developed for storage that suits the store's requirements. Storage by age and sex saves space and makes it easy to find the mannequin needed without loss of time. Ideally, a separate compartment is provided for each mannequin. If this is not possible, a separate shelf for arms, hands, and wig is usually provided. The sketch illustrates one arrangement that is inexpensive and practical.

Rough pine is a good material for shelving. It can be supplemented with cloth or felt to protect the finish of the mannequins. This area should be vacuum cleaned regularly.

Women's mannequins are dressed much as a real person would be. Therefore the displayman can stand to work. Exceptions to this are slacks, some skirts, swimwear, intimate apparel and shoes. The mannequin must be "broken" at the waist for this merchandise. The point is that a chair and a rack may be sufficient furniture in the dressing area if women's mannequins are the only type used.

If children's mannequins are in our displayman's repertoire they must be dressed closer to eye-level so that the displayman will not have to bend constantly and so that he will see his work more as it will appear when finished.

With any shirt or blouse form (one representing the torso only), eye-level work is mandatory. Since they are almost always used with "soft" lines, a worktable adjacent to the mannequin bin should be reserved for pinning. Ideally this should have a cloth cover. A turntable is a very useful device, either purchased or improvised, so that the work can be turned easily while pinning.

Men's mannequins present special problems. They can be placed horizontally on a chair or worktable for pulling on the trousers and shoes. A short-cut that many displaymen prefer (this is too heavy for the girls to try) because it's quick and prevents wrinkling the trousers is to stand the men mannequins on their heads. After the trousers and shoes are on, the rest of the job is done with the mannequin in a standing position.

In any dressing operation care must be taken to prevent scuffing the soles of shoes, the top of the men mannequins heads, and all other exposed parts of the mannequin. For this reason, a space should be reserved with a carpet or cloth cover where the dressing is done. Just a two-foot square can be adequate. The important thing is to develop good habits. As mannequins are dressed they can be stood on paper to protect the shoes or masking tape can be stripped on the soles. All of this discussion assumes that the mannequins are dressed at the "bin" or adjacent to the storeroom. If the particular store situation requires that dressing be done in the windows or at the display site, the same general rules for care of the mannequins should apply. More on this later.

4. How much space in the display shop should be allocated for painting? This, like prop building, will vary widely from store to store. If a neutral grey, white, or black is used for fixtures, seasonal color can be picked up in foliage or signs, thus cutting painting to a minimum,

possibly only that necessary to keep the fixtures clean. At the other extreme, some stores find it desirable to paint fixtures and props with almost every change. Neither is wrong but a very different allocation of shop space is necessary.

In the first case, it may be enough to take the fixtures onto the roof and spray them with paint from an aerosol can. In the second case, it will be worth while to have built a special spray booth equipped with exhaust fans, air compressors and spray guns.

In laying out shop space for painting, we are, of course, talking about spray painting and not the preparation of murals. Murals are very effective display backgrounds painted with tempera colors, chalk or India ink on seamless paper. It is a good idea to reserve a wall in the shop where this can be done. It must be at least 8 feet high (to accommodate the width of a seamless paper roll) and be where the artist can stand back from his work from time to time.

In every plan for painting, proper ventilation and the elimination of fire hazards are primary. Never attempt to spray paint in an enclosed area without proper vents. The advice of experts should be obtained for safeguarding all painting areas.

5. A sign of some sort is an essential part of almost every display. Serious thought should be given to the place where they are made. In larger stores the sign shop is in a separate room with the sign shop manager coming under the general supervision of the display manager. The equipment will vary from large sign machines, silk screen process equipment, and offset presses in the larger stores to a speedball pen in the smallest shop.

Sign shop routine boils down to a requisition of some sort, either oral or written, the actual production, and return of the sign to the place where it will be used. Even the smallest shop will follow a similar routine. The physical layout should facilitate the accomplishment of these tasks.

To prevent salespersons from interfering with production, a "mail box" of some sort is necessary where they can leave requisitions. Wherever possible, this should be inserted in a wall so that the requisition can be delivered without entering the work area, and so the sign maker can easily place the completed sign in the box.

To understand the importance of a "mail box," we must understand that the sign shop in most retail operations does not produce just window "readers" and signs used in display areas under the direct control of the display manager, but makes merchandise cards and size and price tickets used by every department in the store. Without a

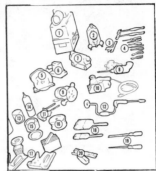

Fig. 17   Shown here are some of the basic equipment of the versatile display shop. The items are identified according to the code numbers on the sketch. 1. Delineascope 2. Cutawl 3. Square 4. Group of hand tools: 2 hammers, 2 screw drivers, putty knife, paper cutter, pliers, wire cutters 5. Skilsaw 6. Finish sander 7. Rough sander 8. Electric drill 9. Router 10. Jigsaw 11. Gauge for router 12. Brace and bit 13. Plastic wood 14. Glue 15. Friction and cellophane tape 16. Wire 17. Staple guns and staples 18. Paint brushes 19. Wood Chisel 20. Staple clipper.

Fig. 18   Cutawl in operation.

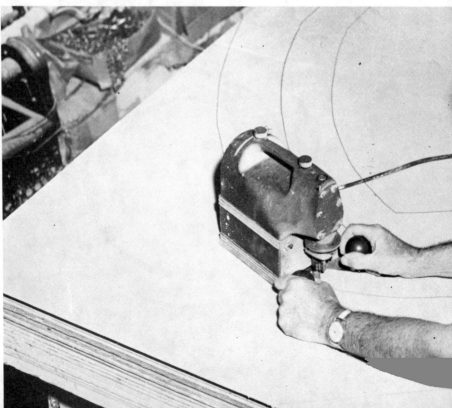

Fig. 19   The bench saw in operation.

Fig. 20   Example of cutout panels possible with Cutawl machine.

physical separation between the sign maker and the requisitioners, production will suffer.

The sketch shows one idea for the sign area in a display shop in a medium sized department store with approximately $1,800,000 annual gross volume. For purposes of illustration, it will be assumed that it is operated by one full-time person.

Sign making will be discussed in more detail in a later chapter, but for now, when our concern is only for the physical layout of the display shop (of which the sign shop is an important part), note the following important characteristics:

a. There is provision for machine-made, hand-lettered, or cut-out letter signs.

b. The sign operator's desk is near the mailbox so he can sort requisitions easily.

c. There is adequate provision for trash. A fire-proof, covered receptacle is a must since solvents, etc., used in sign making are highly inflammable.

d. There is an outlet for water.

e. A paper cutter is provided.

f. Card storage areas are close to the machine or table where they will be used.

g. There is a "home" for everything. The layout eliminates waste motion.

6. An important fact for beginning displaymen to understand is that the display staff are not the only persons who will handle display fixtures. Every person in the store will have occasion to handle them. Adequate storage and the cooperation of management in enforcing their proper use is an imperative part of planning the layout of the display shop.

A few general points on the subject of fixture storage may be helpful as it applies to stands, shelf hardware, glass, price ticket holders, sign holders, and a dozen and one other small items that are not the exclusive responsibility of the display staff. These are handled by the entire store personnel but must be stored in the display shop.

a. In the first place, take a hard look at each item's real function. If it isn't directly related to merchandise presentation it should be stored in another area. Light bulbs are a good example. Too often, not only display bulbs like colored fluorescents, but bulbs for the entire building are stored in the display shop.

b. Have storage shelves built in a wide range of height and depth.

c. Insist that as many items as possible be broken down for storage.

For example, blouse forms can be stored on one shelf and their stands in an adjacent shelf. This will save much space.

d. Prohibit (with the possibility of reprimand or even dismissal for repeated infractions) the placement of any kind of display fixture under counters, in empty drawers, or tucked away behind doors in any area except the display storage area.

e. Have the shelves clearly marked so that inexperienced persons can see where things go.

INEXPENSIVE DISPLAY MATERIALS

The following list does not pretend to be exhaustive. It will summarize some of the categories that are in widespread use.

1. *Wood:* Soft pine is the most easily worked wood for general display use. The most valuable size, 1 by 2 inches, can be used for frames to support composition board or paper, assembled in geometric designs (a la Mondrian), and sprayed with paint they make a good background without covering, and they serve a multitude of general utility purposes.

Some displaymen like to keep a stock of lath in their store room. This can be sprayed in seasonal colors (especially during the spring and Easter seasons), assembled in various lattice combinations, or bent to make very handsome backgrounds. Wood that has been molded into circles, ovals, etc., is available from display manufacturers and can be used alone or combined with bent lath by the imaginative displayman for striking effects.

Fine woods, such as mahogany, oak and walnut have a place in display work. Fixtures made with them are of a permanent or semi-permanent character and are purchased from display manufacturers. Rich veneers, along with brass, are old standbys in men's-wear shops. Less expensive, but also less attractive substitutes can be had in wood-grained paper.

Wood (or metal) is better than composition materials for shelves of any sort if the weight to be carried is considerable. Many an otherwise attractive display has come to grief because it sagged after a short time. The abnormal heat in display windows will cause papers and cardboards to warp, shrink, bend and otherwise misbehave. If there is any doubt about the weight of the objects or the effect of heat in the window, well seasoned wood (or metal) should be used.

Natural birch, bamboo, yucca poles and manzanita branches are very useful props. Some can be obtained locally by resourceful displaymen or they can be purchased. Rugs are usually rolled with bamboo poles for support. Department store display managers might ask the rug department to save the poles. Manzanita mounted on a base is widely used for jewelry displays.

2. *Batting:* Ethereal effects are achieved with batting or spun glass, along with proper lighting. Clouds, space scenes, etc., can be made with spun glass. It is sometimes used on the window floor so that the mannequins appear to be floating. Spun glass is rather expensive and does not lend itself to re-use.

For inexpensive, more routine use Dacron polyester batting is a good material. It can be pinned into any desired shape; it can be re-used, and it is extremely light and white. Cotton batting is even less expensive but does not possess the beautiful appearance of Dacron.

3. *Ribbon:* Satin or acetate ribbons in seasonal colors and several widths have many uses in the construction of backgrounds, for gift-wrapped boxes, for suspending merchandise, etc. Try suspending evenly spaced ribbon across the back of the window for an inexpensive, high fashion treatment for ready-to-wear, infant's or children's windows. Ribbon is now available with flexible wire reinforcement with a multitude of uses.

4. *Seamless Paper:* Rolls up to 107 in. by 50 ft. can be purchased in a wide range of colors. It is inexpensive and very useful in providing seasonal color on walls, flats, table tops and for painting window background murals. It is probably less expensive and easier to change than paint. On the minus side, it tends to cheapen the display if used excessively or carelessly. Some people like to let the ends of the roll curl like a manuscript while others prefer to tear the edge in a deckle effect, and still others prefer to tack all the edges neatly out of sight on the back side of the table top, flat, or what-ever (take extra pains to achieve neatness at the corners). This is a matter of experimentation and is usually determined by the nature of the display.

5. *Rubber Base Paint:* Most displaymen prefer rubber base paints to oil paints for general use because it is quick drying and dries mat. Paint is used for more permanent changes, while paper or cloth is used for more routine changes. It's a good idea to keep some of the wall color to cover nicks that inevitably occur when lots of merchandise goes in and out of the window.

6. *Aerosol Spray Paints:* These are fairly expensive, but a limited number for touch-up on fixtures are very handy. Glossy lacquers and metallics are currently popular for achieving antique and art nouveau effects. Spray paints are also available in flesh colors for touch-up on mannequins. The extent of their use is usually in direct proportion to the total amount of painting required by the display department.

7. *Wallboard:* This is sold under several trade names of which Upson is probably the best known. It is useful for construction of flats, small tables, and cut-out designs and letters. The last use is usually not practical for small shops unless they wish to undertake the expense of a Cutawl or similar machine. A good display wallboard should be strong; it should cut and drill easily and smoothly; it should be lightweight; both sides should be usable; and it should provide a good painting surface. Most boards are sold in 4 by 8-foot sizes and 1/8 or 3/16-inch thicknesses.

8. *Hand Tools:* One can get by very well with just a few tools. The most important are: Diagonal cutters or "nippers" (for cutting pins or wire), a staple gun, a small hammer, paper shears, a pin cushion (attached to a wrist band, attached to a belt holder, or used separately), dress-maker pins, banker pins (the heavier sizes will substitute for nails), paper clips, casein glue, masking tape, fishing leader (instead of wire because it is transparent), and tie wire.

9. *Power Tools:* There isn't a power tool that cannot be replaced with a hand tool if necessary. A coping saw will do the work of a Cutawl, sandpaper will do the work of a sanding machine, etc. Therefore the choice of hand or power tools for the display shop must depend on the amount of each operation that will be done. Everything in the shop (including the displayman) must pay its way or be replaced, is a practical rule.

If only one power tool could be purchased, first choice of many shops would no doubt be a Cutawl. This is the trade name of a machine to cut intricate designs in wallboard, wood, plastic or thin metals. It is equipped with a variety of blades and chisels for different materials. The operator guides it by means of two ball handles. It is more versatile and rugged than a saber saw. At a price under $200 (plus attachments) it is worth the consideration of all stores that do any prop building.

A power-driven bench saw with tilting arbor permits the display shop to cut lumber, plastics or wallboard with a great saving of time and effort.

Other power tools that are worthy of consideration are disk and belt sanders, band saws and drill presses.

10. *Floor Coverings:* One of the least expensive materials is seamless paper cut into tiny pieces. Ends of rolls can be utilized this way. Grass mats can be purchased for spring and summer displays or grass-like scatter materials can be used. Shredded plastic in white (for snow) or colors makes colorful displays. Other materials are cork, colored "match-sticks," stone, the "holes" from pegboard, button

Fig. 21

THE BOLD
AND THE BEAUTIFUL

FROM OUR FASHION FLOOR ON

Fig. 22

Fig. 23

scraps, and many others. If you're stuck for a floor cover and the display really seems to need color in this area, try a small scatter rug in the appropriate color, borrowed from the home furnishings department. This isn't recommended as a crutch for inefficiency, but should be reserved for emergencies, partly because the rug will almost always have to be marked down.

MANNEQUINS

In recent years, and largely through the influence of European displaymen, there has developed a minor tendency to replace mannequins with abstract clothing forms and flexible wire fixtures. Even with this influence, the life-like mannequin will probably survive the competition. Nothing can really replace it for showing the end use of a garment, that is to say, how it will look on.

Mannequin construction has changed radically with technological development. At one time wax was used for their construction. This scratched easily and was easily damaged by temperature changes. Wax was replaced with papier mache. Many of these are in use today. Papier mache mannequins are covered with fiber and the outer "skin" consists of lacquer. Papier mache mannequins are gradually being replaced by plastic. Manufacturers and displaymen alike agree on its superior resistance to moisture, heat and scuffing.

Women and children's mannequins are equipped with a rod and base to make them stand. The base is usually metal but can be ordered in glass. (This varies with the manufacturer.) Glass has the advantage of permitting the carpet to show as an uninterrupted area in the design. Male mannequins usually do not have stands. They are fitted with an adjustable bolt in the heels that maintain their balance. New women's figures for slacks, ski pants, etc. have this same fitting.

Mannequins are made in standing, sitting, reclining, and various novelty poses. A word of caution for the beginning displayman! Be certain to have sufficient standing figures, selected with an eye to their ability to "wear clothes" rather than the novelty of their pose, before investing in the less orthodox models.

Some of the common causes of rapid mannequin deterioration are 1. failure to tighten bolts on the rod and base. Looseness causes the material to breakdown and eventually the entire rod socket will break away. 2. Moving the mannequin completely assembled. They should always be taken apart for moving from one area to another. 3. Changing shoes on dressed mannequins by lifting them on the rod. This occurs because the displayman didn't think about the choice of shoes or because they are sold. The cure for the first is obvious. In the second case, a good policy is to reserve shoes by putting a note on the back of the window door. Very few women will object to this if the shoe clerk explains it in a courteous manner. 4. Failure to clean the mannequin regularly. 5. Inadequate storage areas.

Wigs for women's and children's mannequins were traditionally made with horsehair, but nylon and other synthetics are coming to the fore. They are removable and are the only part of the mannequin that should be changed with another. The arms and hands are designed as integral parts of the whole, therefore should never be traded with those of a different gesture or design. If the serial numbers are sent to the manufacturer, he can usually make exact replacements for broken hands and arms.

Men mannequins usually are not made with wigs. The hair is indicated by modelling and paint. Experimentation is underway constantly to remedy this situation.

An important consideration that is often overlooked is a regular, systematic inventory of the mannequin bin. Too many obsolete and damaged mannequins and forms are retained. This makes it difficult to work, causes damage to good mannequins by taking space, causes arms, wigs and bases to become hopelessly confused, and most important, prevents the systematic use of a budget for mannequin replacement.

No doubt this attitude of hanging onto everything, even if it is out-of-date, dirty and broken, comes from the fact that hard experience has taught displaymen that dollars to buy new equipment may not be forthcoming. On the other hand, failure to clean-out old equipment results in loss of time, damage to good mannequins, and sloppy work, all un-economical practices in themselves.

This does not mean that the "bin" must be stocked with only new mannequins. A step-down system is employed with great success in many departments. Some mannequins are in an "A" category. These are used in the windows and the most important interior display areas. A "B" group is refinished and fitted with new wigs to be used in less important displays. A "C" group is designated for use in building props, as "loaners" to schools and churches (if it is the store policy to loan at all), and for hand and wig replacements.

When the time comes for a regular inventory, mannequins in the "C" group are the first to go into the trash (actually, very few need to be completely discarded. Mannequin refinishing companies will pay a small amount for them or give an allowance on refinishing bills). Some in the "B" group will have deteriorated and are stepped-down to the "C" group; some in "A" will move to "B," and a few new replacements will be purchased. In this way a well rounded inventory is maintained.

It is possible to amortize the cost of mannequins over a five-year period and predict with accuracy how much budget will be required for a fresh line of mannequins and fixtures at all times. This will prevent ups and downs in store appearance. Have you ever heard anyone say "——— Store had nice displays when they first opened but they're awful now"? Chances are they used their original equipment, without maintenance, until it was a shambles. When replacement was finally undertaken, the store would have been faced with a whopping big expenditure, all coming from one year's operation.

Mannequins are designed to wear clothing in all of the popular size ranges. The following chart gives an idea of the mannequins in common use (sizes vary slightly depending upon the manufacturer):

GROUP	SIZE	SHOE SIZE	
Infant	6 mos. to 1 year, seated or reclining		9 (infant)
Toddler	2 years, boy or girl		9½
Toddler	4 years, boy or girl		5½ D
Toddler	3 years, boy or girl		6½ D
Children	6 years, boy or girl		7 D
Children	8 years, boy or girl		10 C
Children	10 years, boy or girl		12 C
Children	12 years, boy or girl	13½ C	2 C
Children	18 months	(girl)	(boy)
		2 C	4 C
		(girl)	(boy)
Teen	Pre-teen 10 or 12		3 B
Teen	Teen girl 12 (difference in teen figures is not only size, but largely make-up)		3 B
Teen	16 years, boy (boy and men mannequins fitted with supplementary wooden arms for action poses)		5 C
Teen	18 years, boy		6 C
Women	Junior Petite, sizes 5 to 13 (wears size 7 or 9) models clothing for 5'7" and under group)		5 B
Women	Junior, sizes 5 to 15 (wears size 9 or 11)		5 B
Women	Half Sizes, sizes 14½ to 44½ (wears size 14½) models clothing for elderly and stout women		5½ B
Women	Misses, sizes 10 to 18 (wears 10 with straight skirt or slacks; 12 with full skirt)		5½ B
Men	Suit size 40 regular Shirt size 15½-32		8½

43

Fig. 25

Fig. 26

All-Weather Coats

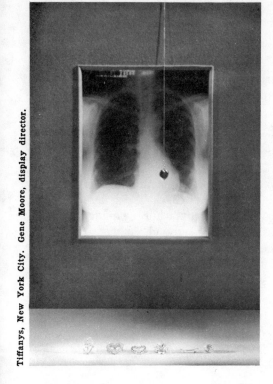

Tiffanys, New York City. Gene Moore, display director.

chapter 4

always start with merchandise

A SUCCESSFUL display is the sum of several successful parts. An orchestra is a useful analogy. The music will not be good if each musician is not proficient with his instrument, no matter how masterful the composition. Display composition is the blending together of merchandise units, the background, selling messages and lighting. Just as each player in the orchestra must strive to master his instrument, the displayman must be able to groom and form any merchandise in the store before he can compose it in a finished way.

Any merchandise must be groomed for display. What are the verbs that describe this process? To press, to brush, to wash, to dust, to polish, are but a few. Of these, to press is the most important to stores that handle so-called soft lines. A few general considerations about pressing that may be helpful to beginners are:

1. Pressing time is never wasted because it is made up by the ease with which the trim can be completed. Many inexperienced persons

45

will spend more time tugging and pulling at wrinkles than it would take to return the merchandise to the pressing room to be pressed properly.

2. Nothing, even beautiful foliage and high-priced props . . can substitute for or justify unpressed merchandise.

3. The higher priced department stores and specialty shops are often the worst offenders regarding pressing while the popular price shops often do the best work.

4. Most stores steam merchandise before it leaves the stock room. In some cases, blankets and bedspreads for example, steaming is adequate grooming.

5. Pressing is sometimes done by the displayman. In other cases it is done by tailor shop personnel. In the latter case, the displayman must acquaint the presser with his requirements. For example, he will probably explain that sleeves are pressed round, or he may want trousers with "quick" (unfinished edge folded under) instead of regular cuffs. In any case, he should try to develop an attitude of pride in the presser, to make the presser know that the display's success is partly his accomplishment.

6. A steam iron is the basic tool used in tailor shops. In addition, most shops have Hoffman type presses, i.e., boards that close on a clamshell principle. Various shaped boards and steam heads are also used.

PINNING AND GROOMING TECHNIQUES

Clothing forms are offered to the displayman in such variety that there is little need for altering them, provided they are up-to-date, are the right size, and in reasonably good condition. In case alteration of the form is necessary it is done by adding tissue paper, suit wadding or cardboards.

Generally speaking, glass and plastic fixtures are more suitable for feminine displays while metal or wood are best with masculine displays. There is no hard rule, except that it is better not to mix the two in close proximity.

A basic trick that every displayman should know is how to lock a pin. To prevent the annoyance of a pin that won't hold, push it through three thicknesses, reverse it, then push the rest of the pin through, taking care not to expose the pin through the top layer of fabric.

When pins and when staples? Pins are pointed and won't damage merchandise. Even where a pin mark shows, it usually can be removed by gentle pulling and pressing, provided the thread has not been

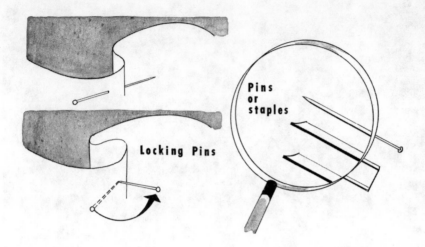

Fig. 27

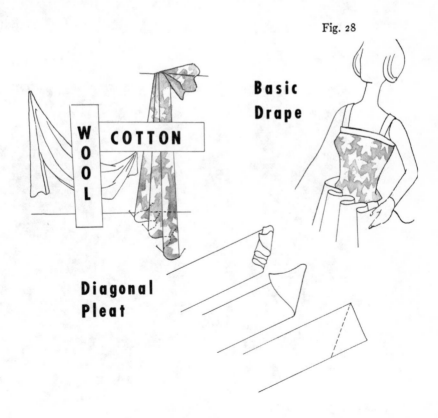

Fig. 28

Basic Drape

WOOL COTTON

Diagonal Pleat

Fig. 29

Fig. 30

broken. Staples are wedge shaped. Therefore, save them for jobs in which re-use of the material is not important.

Tickets to indicate the size and price are placed on merchandise as it enters the store, usually by the stock room personnel. These are attached by pins, strings, or staples. When the merchandise is groomed for display the tickets must be concealed but never thrown away. If the merchandise will be seen only from the front, the tickets can be pinned at the back. A uniform system for concealing tickets will save time.

Probably the best advice for learning display tricks is to study competition. Make it a regular habit to visit other stores. Look behind things, when this is possible, to see where pins are placed. What follows are just a few basic tricks with specific lines that will be helpful.

SHOP TRICKS WITH SPECIFIC LINES

1. *Piece Goods:* In handling yardage, either for backgrounds or as the featured merchandise, cottons will look best if the folds are pulled tight and pinned. Woolens and silk look best draped in soft, flowing lines. Either category is pleated to about ¼ its width for display purposes. The pleats in cotton are pulled to the floor and pinned, a pin being necessary at both the front and back of each fold.

Yardage used in display is usually sold as remnants after the display is removed. Therefore lengths should be cut that can be sold. For example, 1 yard of wool will make a skirt. This means that lengths under one yard should not be cut unless they can be written off as display property.

Yardage takes on a richer appearance when it is pleated. There are many ways to do this. The simplest, of course, is to space pleats about 3 inches wide across the width of the piece. Another way is to fold the width diagonally and then pleat along the diagonal. When the entire piece has been gathered in this manner, it is grasped at mid-point and pinned so that both ends drape gracefully.

Yardage displays will be most attractive if color coordinated prints and solids are used together. Manufacturers plan one solid color to match perfectly with three or four prints in the same fabric. The color coordination can be pointed out even more forcefully if the same color thread, bias tape, or other notions are worked into the display as accessories.

European displaymen are masters of yardage displays, and especially mannequin draping. While apprentice displaymen do not need to possess this skill in a high degree, it is well to know at least one basic way to drape a mannequin. A mannequin draped in the featured fabric shows the *end use* and adds drama to the display.

First, a foundation must be provided so that extensive pinning can be done without damaging the mannequin. An inexpensive cotton slip is good for this. The easiest drape is possibly a sundress style (also adaptable as a formal by omitting the straps and letting the skirt come to the floor). In this drape the yardage is pleated and pinned until the skirt is complete. The bodice is of the same piece, folded on the center and trimmed with pieces in a coordinated color.

A shirtwaist style can be created with about 4 and ½ yards of fabric by bringing the fabric across the left shoulder, continuing over the other shoulder, pinning the excess out of sight at the back and forming sleeves by pinning the excess at the back of the arms, and then completing the drape by pinning and pleating the rest of the fabric around the waist to form the skirt.

Finish the drapes by adding an appropriate belt, flower, piece of jewelry or other accessory. With practice it is possible to keep all the pins to the back and out of sight. If an occasional pin does have to be used in front, it can sometimes be hidden by the careful placement of an accessory. All edges should be folded under as the draping progresses to give a neat, finished look.

2. *Women's Ready-to-Wear:* Fundamental to trimming ready-to-wear is learning to dress a mannequin. Most clothing stores stock merchandise that is packed in plastic bags (slips, blouses, sweaters, etc.). A few of these should be held as merchandise is opened for display to cover the mannequin wigs when garments are pulled on. Never try to pull a garment over the wig. Either remove the wig or cover it.

It will be noted that mannequins are designed to simulate the walk or stance of a real person. The left arm is forward when the left foot is back and vice versa. To reverse this makes the mannequin appear awkward. On the other hand, do not push the arms into exaggerated gestures unless the reason for the gesture is clear and important to the display.

If the garment has any excess fabric, turn the folds away from the line of sight. See your trims from the customer's point-of-view. With care, all evidence of pinning can be concealed.

The belt on a dress should point to the right as you look at it and be set in the second hole. The excess belt, like the excess fabric, is folded over, away from the customer's line of sight, and held with a large paper clip. Always check to be certain that the belt is centered.

After the garment has been pinned, the hem line must be checked. This can only be done by getting down on the floor or going outside the window. The hem line should come to the length prescribed by the prevailing fashion. This will usually be a problem only if the dress

Fig. 31   Fig. 32

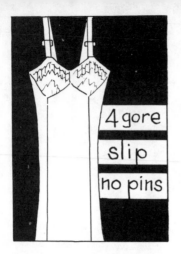

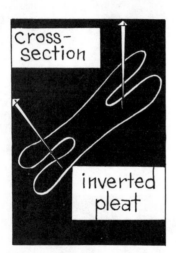

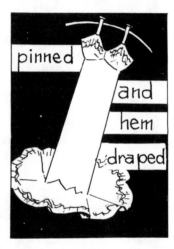

Fig. 33

Fig. 34

is smaller or larger than the mannequin size. Finally, check the garment closely for loose threads. These will usually hang down below the hem and are not apt to be noticed while the work is in progress. Rest assured that they will look like magnified spaghetti to the customer standing outside the window.

3. *Women's Furnishings:* If one can pin a slip for display, it is possible to handle any other garment in the women's furnishing line in an attractive way. The first step, after careful pressing, is to shorten the straps. Then the slip is pleated at the bodice. The panels in slips are called gores. There are two and four gore slips. A four gore slip pleats along the seams as shown in the illustration. A two gore slip pleats the same way except that the seams cannot be used as a guide. Then the front panel is lifted slightly to give a bloused effect to the bodice. A pin is inserted from the back, through all four thicknesses. Two more pins are used to hold the back of the slip to the front at the origin of the shoulder straps.

The slip can be draped by swirling the hem and following the folds caused by swirling, or it can be draped, straps down, from a stand. Slips have a lighter, more feminine appearance if they are pinned and draped than if they are displayed on mannequins.

Hosiery drapes should emphasize the sheerness of the fabric. This is done by slightly overlapping several hose, each following the same general line. This is known as "fanning." This type of display is shown in conjunction with hosiery on leg forms. The "fan" shows the sheerness and catches the eye, while the leg form points out the details.

4. *Foundations and Maternity Wear:* The matter of taste enters more into the display of intimate garments than in any other line. Two general principles may help one to adhere to the generally accepted standards of good taste.

First, the use of abstract clothing forms shows the end use of the garment without the associations that might be suggested by more realistic mannequins. Second, if mannequins are used, do so with verve. Do not try to hide the fact that the beautiful lady is standing before all the passersby in her undies.

Maternity wear presents similar problems. Some displaymen make the mistake of trying to make the mannequin look as if in the advanced stages of pregnancy. Actually, the expectant mother is looking for garments that will minimize her bulk. Therefore, the practicality of a maternity wear garment should be demonstrated, but made to appear as attractive as possible.

Tulle is an almost indispensable item for trimming personal garments. This is a nylon net material in many colors that can be ruffled, pleated and draped to soften the edges of any feminine trim. It is so widely used that a study of competition windows will reveal many techniques for its use.

5. *Sportswear:* What to do with sleeves seems to be the most common question posed by beginners. There is no problem if a blouse or sweater is shown on a mannequin, because the arms fill them out. But on a blouse form or stand, sleeves have a limp, unattractive appearance.

Short sleeves are pinned to the form so the sleeve forms a neat triangle. Long sleeves are pinned to the form just below the mid-point in the sleeve. The rest of the sleeve can be draped on the floor or other supporting surface, or it can be lifted and the cuff pinned to the form. The entire long sleeve can also be pleated and pinned at the shoulder. A tissue paper roll is sometimes helpful if the sleeve requires more body.

Experienced displaymen save clean, corrugated packing boxes for pinning boards. The board is trimmed with a mat knife to the approximate shape of a skirt, slacks, shorts, or whatever garment is to be formed. A judicious exaggeration of the shape can sometimes bring out important characteristics of the merchandise. If the garment is sheer, a white cardboard can be added to the brown corrugated board. The pressed garment is smoothed carefully on the pinning board and the excess fabric is pulled to the back and pinned, always with the pin pointed in the direction of pull to insure against slipping.

This technique is not only good with sportswear but is suitable with any merchandise that can be shown flat. By tilting and elevating the completed boards in various angles, the display suggests animation.

6. *Millinery:* Millinery heads, plastic or metal stands, topped with sponge rubber or tissue, or wooden dowels are all good millinery fixtures. Wooden dowels are drilled and mounted on finishing nails that can be driven into the display floor.

Tulle or colored tissue paper is often used around the base of millinery fixtures to soften the effect of the unadorned stand. Artificial or real flowers are used as a prop in spring displays so that the hat appears to be another flower.

The keys to effective millinery arrangements are *grouping by color* and *variety in direction and elevation.* A woman almost always "shops" a millinery display by color. She is looking for the color that goes with a particular outfit. A whole table of one color, then another table featuring another color, and so on, will really command attention.

Variety in millinery displays is achieved by using fixtures at various levels and by turning the hats. Think of yourself as the customer before starting every trim. Ask yourself "What's important about this merchandise?" In the case of millinery, the back or side or even the lining

Fig. 35

Fig. 36

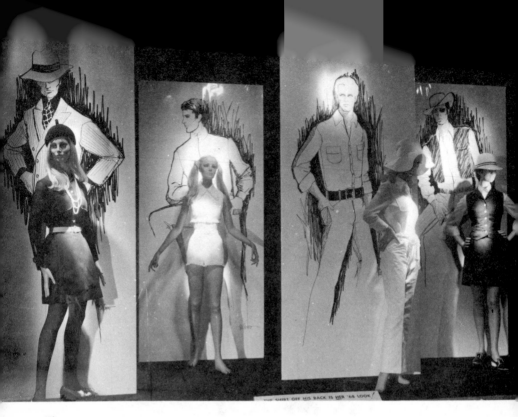

THE SHIRT OFF HIS BACK IS HER '68 LOOK

Fig. 37

Fig. 38

April Showers
YOUNG THINGS
SIXTH FLOOR

Ohrbach's

Fig. 39

Fig. 40

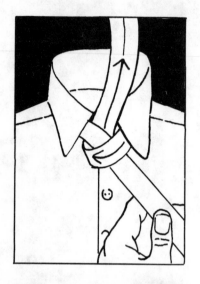

Fig. 41

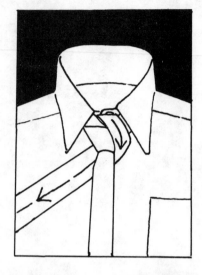

Fig. 42

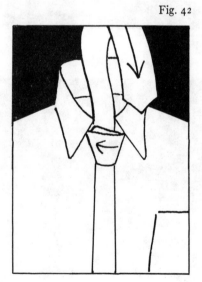

may be the important selling point. If so, don't hesitate to turn it to expose the most sales appealing points. Other examples of turning are women's coats if there is an especially attractive detail, or shoes, if the heel is outstanding.

7. *Children's Clothing* (infants and girls): This manual does not pretend to describe every technique for trimming every line. However, with children's clothing, and sometimes with other departments, stuffing with tissue paper is an effective method.

Tissue paper should be the only kind of paper used because heavier weights will show wrinkles through the cloth. The idea is to show animation by turning, bending, and pinning the garment in various ways. Try to recall the typical gestures of children in school or play. Jeans, pedal-pushers, creepers, etc., lend themselves particularly well to this kind of trim.

A careful selection of sizes to match the mannequins is important with every age group but especially critical with children's mannequins. A few pins can usually compensate for the wrong size in a woman's dress. The tolerance is not so great in children's lines.

8. *Men's and Boys' Wear:* Learning to dress (or "rig," as the men's wear trimmers say) a suit form is fundamental to this merchandise category.

First, it is very difficult to do a good job on an old-fashioned form. It can be done, but lots of suit wadding, tissue, pins, and skill are necessary. It's much easier if the suit coat has been neatly pressed and if the jersey-covered suit form is designed for the modern silhouette in men's wear.

Detailed instructions on men's neckties may be found in specialized manuals. A basic knot that must be mastered by every displayman is the full Windsor. It is tied as shown in the numbered diagrams.

1. Form a simple knot by bringing the large end over the small and up behind.

2. Bring the big end over the opposite side and under.

3. Carry the big end over and down behind the knot.

4. The knot will form a triangle at this point. Bring the big end across the face of the triangle, then behind and up over the knot, then down through the top two layers.

5. Adjust the dimple while pulling snug. Hold the small end with the left hand and the knot with the right. Slide the knot into place in the collar.

Most suit forms are designed to wear a 40 regular jacket. After tieing the necktie, the shirt must be pinned so that no wrinkles will show in the exposed part, the sleeves are tucked out of sight in the holes at the shoulder (some stores carry the sleeve through the coat sleeve so that about ½ in. of cuff shows), and the excess material is gathered at the back and pinned in two bi-symmetrical folds. Some displaymen use shirt dickies instead of shirts from stock for rigging suit forms. The men's department manager will usually prefer this because it will eliminate mark-downs on the shirts used for display. On the other hand, actual inspection of the cost will show that the tiny amount of mark-down necessary is greatly offset by the increased volume created by effective display.

To make the suit coat adhere to the form as though it was "poured," attach thin cardboards cut with scissors to match the contour of the coat hem, to the bottom of the suit form. The coat is then placed on the form and carefully centered.

Sleeve pads are inserted and pinned at the shoulder. Later, they will be pinned to the suit form near the cuff so that no air shows between the form and sleeve. Expert men's wear "riggers" take pride in achieving this sleeve position without pinning.

Sleeve pads are a matter of debate among displaymen. Some prefer full pads while others prefer a very light pad or even a mere roll of tissue. In general, the modern silhouette in men's wear indicates light sleeve padding. It is possibly best to make your own pads by stapling suit wadding and tissue to a cardboard cut to conform to the sleeve shape. Excellent ready-made pads are also available.

After centering the coat, it is anchored to the form by placing pins under the lapels. Then the "rigging" proceeds by running the hand gently from top to bottom of the coat and pinning the lining to the cardboard that has already been attached to the form. This is rather hard to describe. The object is to make the coat conform as closely as possible without trace of wrinkles, and to anchor this conformity by pinning to the cardboard. A real understanding of the process can only be gained by actually doing it. With practice, one can place pins so they will not show and yet be firmly anchored in the thin cardboard.

Of course, no amount of rubbing, pinning, and stuffing will substitute for sloppy pressing. The old saying that a good beginning will insure a good ending certainly applies in preparing men's suits for display. People are sometimes surprised to learn that they are one of the hardest garments to display well. The slightest wrinkle, sloppy pinning, etc., will show up like a sore thumb in the finished display.

Pinning a man's shirt is similar in principle to pinning a suit. The perfectly pressed shirt is brought into closer comformity with the shirt form through pinning. The order of pinning a shirt can be described as a capital T. The first pin is placed at the collar. The second and third pins anchor the yoke to the form at the shoulders. The fourth pin holds the front center of the shirt to the form near the bottom button.

At this point, the displayman should inspect his work closely before proceeding. If the shirt does not make a perfect T, he will have trouble with the rest of the pinning. Sometimes cheap shirts won't make perfect T's simply because of sloppy cutting. This simply illustrates the fact that the most skillful displaymen sometimes work in the lowest priced shops. Succeeding pins are placed out of sight into the under edge of the form along its base. Before each pin is placed the fabric is smoothed with the hand from top to the bottom near the point where the pin will go.

The excess material is gathered at the back of the shirt and pinned in two box-pleats, arranged bi-symmetrically. The back of the shirt tail is usually lifted slightly and pinned so that it will not be seen from the front.

Shirt tails can be arranged by lifting slightly at the seams and pinning so that they are perfectly bi-symmetrical when seen from the front. It is sometimes a good idea to add small cardboards under the shirt tails to give them a crisp look.

Long-sleeved shirts are pinned to the lower edge of the form slightly below the mid-point of the seam so that no air shows between the sleeve and the body of the shirt.

If a more decorative sleeve treatment is desired, it should not distort the garment in a way to detract from its masculine character. A commonly used decorative treatment is called a triangle point. It is made by moving the sleeve to the back and pinning the seam near the back of the yoke. The rest of the fabric and cuff are "puffed" and the folds held by pins. Sometimes one sleeve is handled decoratively and the other is pinned naturally. If the shirt has one pocket, the decorative treatment should be used on the side opposite the pocket. Also, a window or department with several shirt forms should follow a uniform system for the sake of unity and greater visual impact.

Many of the pins used in display work can be hidden by clipping the heads with diagonal cutters and then pulling the fabric over the end of the clipped pin. Concealing pins by clipping is especially useful in grooming men's wear. A pin will hold even after the head has been clipped and it is out of sight. Experienced trimmers always have their diagonal cutters handy. These are also known as "dikes" or "nippers."

Putting mannequin arms into their sockets without wrinkling the merchandise is difficult. The secret is 1. to keep everything unbuttoned until the arms are in place, 2. to put one arm (minus the hand) on the mannequin and then slide the garment or garments (a shirt and outer garment, such as a coat, for example) over the arm. Then the second arm (again minus the hand) is inserted through the sleeve from the top. With one hand reach into the sleeve cuff to guide the arm, and with the other hand hold the arm at the shoulder to guide it into the socket. Avoid grasping the merchandise with a tight squeeze at anytime during this process. A nervous person's hand will be warm and moist and act like a press wherever the garment is tightly grasped.

9. *Shoes:* Shoes must be carefully groomed. In addition to polishing, the shoe must be filled out or "formed" as it would appear on the foot.

Shoe forms and trees of various kinds can be purchased. They are especially useful with very floppy styles, such as sandals. One type even has a notch to accommodate the thong that goes between the toes. If a shoe form is not used, paper can be stuffed into the shoe to give it the desired form.

When shoes are displayed off mannequins, the shoe lace is not crossed back and forth as one would wear it. Instead, the lace is knotted at one end so it will not slip out of the bottom hole and the knot is hidden inside the shoe. Then the lace is carried across to the opposite hole, through the hole and under the tongue, then up through the next hole on the side where lacing began, across and down, under the tongue, and so on until the lacing is complete. Instead of tieing a bow, the excess lace can be hidden inside the shoe. After the lacing is complete, go back and pull all of the lace up tighter. This kind of lacing has clean lines and is neat because the lace holds the tongue in place.

The shoe department manager will be grateful if the display department is considerate enough to put masking tape on the soles so that they will not be scuffed. The entire sole does not need to be covered. A single strip will provide separation between the sole and floor. The bolt in the heel of men mannequins used to adjust its standing position, should also be taped. A mark will be made on the inside of the shoe if this is not done.

10. *Home Furnishings:* Let's list a few time-tested tricks to get the apprentice over the first hurdles of home furnishings display.

A massive effect is desirable in white goods display. The majority of the sheets should be left in their plastic wrappers. The stacks can be more eye-catching several ways. One is to alternate the angle as the stack is built. Place the first package parallel to the window glass, the next package at a 45 degree angle, the next package parallel, the next at a 45 degree angle, and so on until the stack is complete. If the stacks are built straight, a ribbon and bow around each stack that picks up one of the poster colors will unify the display and give it life. Incidentally, save your energy by "faking" the bows; that is to say, make them in the display shop and pin them to the stacks.

Elevation is a problem with white goods as it is with most displays. If one is not careful everything will be on the floor and nothing will be high enough to be noticed. One or two sheets can be opened and suspended from the ceiling. They should be pressed, just as any other merchandise would be. They can be pleated or suspended as "mountains." To do this, attach a fine wire to one corner of a 72 by 108-inch sheet. Tie the other end of the wire to the ceiling. A variation of this can be achieved inside the store by using a dowel instead of a wire. Check the elevation closely before cutting the wire or dowel. Pin the sheet to the floor after spreading the base so the finished display will resemble an inverted cone or "mountain." A penguin (make one from colored paper or buy one from a display manufacturer) pinned to the mountain will give the display added interest.

When displaying towels leave two folded together. This is the way they are shipped. By leaving them together they will have more body and permit better stacking. Most of the towels can be stacked but a few should be hung over a rod of some sort to give elevation to the display. It is important to show all of the colors available so the shopper will know what will harmonize with her bath room. If matching hand towels and washcloths are available, they should be represented in the display.

Blankets can be stacked, rolled or opened. If they are opened they should be pleated. A rolled blanket can be placed on the floor or stood vertically by inserting a stand in the center of the roll.

The essential in stacking blankets is to have the folded side to the front and to have the sides of the stack even. To do this it is necessary that all of the blankets be folded to the same width. When displaying a two-tone blanket, turn back a corner to show both sides.

The general principles for displaying bedspreads are much the same as for blankets. The chief exception to this general rule is that bedspreads are shown on mock-up beds in complete room ensembles more than blankets. This is because of their style emphasis.

Another device for displaying bedspreads (or table-cloths) is an oval or round wooden frame. The frame is hung vertically and the folds in the suspended spread or table-cloth are arranged bi-symmetrically. This is a good way to show the merchandise on a ledge or perimeter above the department. This technique is good with any item that must be fully opened for the design to be seen.

Curtains and draperies should be hung to look as much as possible as the customer expects them to look in her home. Remember that boards and pins behind the curtain will not show in a window display. This will permit pinning to obtain a crisp effect that would not be possible in actual use.

11. *Jewelry, cosmetics, and small items:* Suppose your manager said, "We intend to use our largest front window to promote a special purchase of wrist watches. I want the display to show only the special purchase watch and it must be a traffic stopper!" This kind of statement is fairly common in department stores. It illustrates one of the problems in displaying small merchandise. Even if the stock is sufficient to build a mass display of one item (it seldom is), the time available to the average displayman working on a tight weekly window change schedule would not be sufficient to do justice to this type of display. What, then, is the solution?

Concentrate on the setting for the merchandise. Don't worry about filling the window. Make the background, the props, the sign, and the lighting fill the window in a way to focus all attention on the promoted item. The "eye-catcher" that fills the largest part of the window may be a cut-out sign, it might be a dynamic poster, it might be a mannequin, or it may be the merchandise alone if the full force of the display light is pinpointed on the featured item.

The day-in, day-out way to promote small items is as accessories with bigger merchandise. Do not think that this is limited to clothing lines, either. To cite just a few examples from the widest range, try writing equipment with back-to-school clothing; drapery hardware with curtains and drapes; cosmetics and perfumes with ladies luggage; gloves, scarfs, caps, etc., with skis; or brushes and rollers with paint. In planning any display try to recall small related items that are sold in your store. The tasteful choice of accessories is not only a way to promote more merchandise, but is the *most effective* way to add interest to the featured item. In fact, many display managers will say that learning to make the proper selection of accessories is one of the most crucial aspects of apprentice training.

12. *Hard Lines:* Two display principles are very apropos of so-called hard lines. These, as the name implies, are furniture, appliances, etc.

First, learn to demonstrate the end use of any merchandise. It may have wonderful qualities plus an outstanding price, but the customer wants to know how it will look on, how it will look in a room ensemble, how it will enhance his person or his standard of living. This is what we mean by demonstrating the end use. Hard lines have taken a cue from the automobile industry. They know that style sells more merchandise than any other single factor. Therefore, the demonstration of the end use in this case will involve an appealing room group.

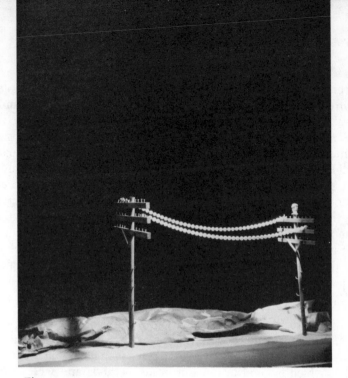

Fig. 43

Fig. 44

Second, your customer can "read" the display easier if plenty of margin is left around its parts. Use a basic shape to build units in a display. This can be a circle, a square, a diamond, or other uniform shape made from wallboard, cork, scatter grass, or other material. Building the display on this shape helps you stay within the margins.

Incidentally, two little tricks will save your temper. Any heavy object suspended on an Upson board background will be more secure if drapery hooks are used instead of pins or nails. Of course, very heavy merchandise should be elevated by building-up from the floor.

The easy way to hang a poster or picture is to use a continuous wire rather than separate wires. Two screweyes on the ceiling grid allow the wire to slide back and forth for minor adjustments. It is very difficult to cut and tie separate wires to the same length.

ABSTRACT AND REALISTIC TRADITIONS

Travelers to Europe have remarked on the contrast in display techniques. Without doubt the Europeans are masterful displaymen. Since World War II there has been a healthy exchange so that we are adopting that which is good in the European methods and vice versa.

In general, the Europeans make better use of fixtures that permit dramatic merchandise effects without the limiting characteristics of mannequins. These fixtures have flexible wire arms, swivel bases, etc. The imaginative displayman can use them to animate the merchandise, suggest end uses, and bring out its innate glamour through skillful draping in a way that is not always possible with mannequins. However, a word of caution to display beginners: These fixtures may look simple in concept and handling but this is misleading. Only an experienced displayman should attempt more elaborate displays with these units, and even they must pay particular attention to achieve hand, arm and body positions that conform to human anatomy.

chapter 5

display composition

G OOD composition is similar in all of the visual arts, including
retail display. (Note that display is correctly called an art.)
The organization of form, color and texture is what underlies good
painting, sculpture, or good display.

One important distinction is the necessity, in retail display, to divide
the job into clearly defined elements. This is necessary partly because
of the physical limitation of working in a restricted space, and partly
by the distinction between the merchandise (or that which is to be
sold), and the background and props (or that which embellishes the
merchandise). If the displayman is not very original or familiar with
his work, it is important for him to complete the following elements in
their proper order, checking each as it is completed for the effect that is
desired in the finished display:

1. *Background:* This term is misleading because it implies something flat on the back wall. It is used for lack of a better term. The

most effective backgrounds create a three dimensional or perspective effect.

2. *The Setup:* This is the arrangement of fixtures and mannequins, that is to say, the things that support the merchandise. The setup can be completed at the display site before any forms or mannequins are dressed or part of the dressing can be done in the display shop. In the last case, the setup must be planned to allow for the forms that will be added. With men's and boys' wear most of the dressing is done in the shop. The setup consists of tables and lifts needed for elevation. In the case of women's clothing and home furnishings more of the dressing is done at the display site.

3. *Major and Minor Merchandise Units:* The setup is planned to accommodate merchandise units. Learn early in the game to think in terms of building units. Do not let merchandise run together without apparent reason.

There can be a major and a minor merchandise unit in the display. Adjacent major units should have a divider between them. Building units will give your displays greater impact, they permit easier movement through windows, and parts of the display can be replaced without disturbing the rest.

4. *Merchandise Accessories:* A unit of two or more accessory items that relate to the major merchandise unit should be planned for every display. It should be a unified composition when seen alone and should become a part of the larger unit. The space occupied by the merchandise accessories will, of course, depend on the number used and their size, but they should be thought of as reinforcing the major merchandise appeal.

5. *Floor Covering or Base:* Some kind of floor covering is an indispensable part of every display composition. It limits the margin of major and minor merchandise units and ties the whole display together.

6. *Reader and Price Tickets:* Space for the reader and price tickets must be planned in every display composition.

BALANCE IN THE DISPLAY

Most important to successful display composition is balance. Placement of the elements listed above in the display area so they will appear unified and not falling in one direction or the other is the essence of good balance.

Good balance is an almost intuitive sense on the part of the displayman so few mechanical rules can apply; however, balance does have some of the qualities of the fulcrum that will illustrate the displayman's

Fig. 45

Fig. 46

Fig. 47

problem. He will have a general guide for the balance of elements if he uses a balance point that can be easily determined. This point is on an imaginary vertical line bisecting the display space. The point selected should correspond to the viewer's natural line of sight. Think of an imaginary horizontal line through this point. Now one imaginary line (vertical) serves as a balance or fulcrum for the elements placed to its right or left and the other imaginary line (horizontal) serves as a balance or fulcrum for the elements placed perpendicularly in the display space. If you're not sure of yourself use the edge of a panel, the top of a table, etc., as real vertical and horizontal lines instead of imaginary lines.

The determination of a balance point is about as much mechanical help as you can get. The rest must depend on a natural sense of element placement that tells you when the display is sufficiently in balance to be attractive and effective.

You can see that application of the "balance point system" in an unimaginative way would result in four more or less related but separate units. They must be tied together, or unified. This is done by careful overlapping of elements in the display, by the intelligent placement of light and dark objects to carry the eye through the display, or by the use of a single color idea in the various elements of the display.

There are two main types of balance. One is called bi-symmetrical or formal. The beginning displayman will do well to use it whenever he is unsure of himself. It is achieved by the placement of equally "weighted" elements on either side of the center. Bi-symmetry is conservative and lends dignity to the merchandise. One should not think from this that it does not have tremendous visual impact. In fact, many displaymen use it for their "sale" windows. Who can deny that a formation of soldiers, airplanes flying in formation, or a chorus line lack visual impact? All are based on similar mechanical systems of visual balance.

The second main type of balance is asymmetrical or informal. This type can be illustrated again by the example of a fulcrum. If one hundred pounds of lead is placed on one side and one hundred pounds of aluminum on the other side of the balance point balance will be achieved but the aluminum will be a much larger mass. The two sides balance but are not the same. In visual phenomena a brighter color, a contrasted value, or an exciting texture will "weigh" more in the total composition than a natural or uninteresting area.

Asymmetrical balance in display is, in general, more interesting than formal balance. Each has its proper place, however, and should be utilized according to the requirements of the specific situation.

The boss doesn't think in terms of symmetrical and asymmetrical balance. If a window display is badly out of balance he will usually see it as a "hole" in the arrangement. He'll say "Joe, can't we fill that 'hole' with more merchandise?" If Joe can't take criticism he will refuse to see that the composition is unbalanced. He will fill the "hole" reluctantly, at the same time cursing all managers for stupid fools. In many cases the problem could have been avoided. The lighter display would have pleased the boss if the displayman had inspected his work more critically for lack of balance.

MORE ASPECTS OF COMPOSITION

1. *Depth:* The displayman works with three dimensions. Depth adds interest to any arrangement. Instead of putting everything on a line, place the display elements at different distances from the spectator or window glass. If an object is pinned flat to a board it will not be as attractive as one that has a little air around it.

Use the side walls if one of your windows is quite deep. As the customer approaches the window from the side he will see more of the side wall than the back wall. Failure to "break-up" the monotony of a large empty wall by the placement of props, merchandise, or even by painting a background, would mean that a deep window could only be seen properly from a stationary position at the exact center of the window. This isn't the way display windows are seen. All displays are seen by walking persons from a variety of angles.

So much for depth where it actually exists. What about creating an illusion of depth when the actual depth is limited? This is done by arranging props and merchandise to give an illusion of perspective or by the controlled use of color and value (see the remarks on the properties of color and value in the last part of this chapter).

Perspective devices to create the illusion of depth break down generally into two types. The first is receding lines that merge at a vanishing point. In display, the merging lines can be created by graphic means (drawing, painting, etc.); they can consist of props (yarn, lath, the angle at which flats are placed, etc.); or the merchandise itself can be placed so that the recession in depth is felt even though an actual line is not visible.

A second perspective device is overlapping objects to give an illusion of depth. For example, a tree trunk, foliage, or other tall object close to the window glass will give the effect of looking into the scene as well as establish scale for the entire display.

2. *Repetition:* Repetition is a valuable device in display composition. So-called "mass" displays are based on this visual principle.

The same item repeated at the same angle throughout the display has an attention-compelling power that is hard to equal by other means. For just one example, a men's shirt promotion might be handled by pinning a large number of folded shirts to a flat. This flat and a sign to set the key for the promotion would be the background. One or two units built around neatly formed shirts (to show the shirt unfolded as well as to indicate the "end use"), plus accessories, reader, and price tickets would complete the composition.

Similarly, one often hears displaymen talk about "banks" of windows. They are thinking of the compositional use of repetition to achieve visual impact. "Bank" in this connection means several windows in which some of the major elements are repeated. The elements would probably be either the background and floor cover, or the major and minor merchandise units. Or the composition of each of several windows might be repeated exactly, with only the color changed in each window. This kind of "bank" is especially apropos with fashion displays.

A mechanical kind of repetition is apt to be monotonous. Therefore the skilled displayman will introduce minor variations in a "bank." Many variations of the principle of repetition are possible. It is as effective with interior displays as with windows. We hear displaymen speak of "banks" of tables, "banks" of shadow boxes, perimeters or platforms. Repetition attracts the eye because it gives both harmony and movement to any display.

An incidental value of repetition which will be dealt with in more detail in a later chapter is that it saves valuable time. Think of the savings if, instead of building a different prop for each window, the same prop can be repeated in several windows!

Removable dividers are a big aid in display composition, particularly as a means of setting up a repeat idea. Instead of dividing windows with permanent side walls, modern stores use dividers that are either suspended from the ceiling grid or set on the floor. A lightweight material such as aluminum is used in much modern construction. They can all be removed if the windows are to be seen as a single unit, they can be equally spaced if the windows are to be handled in "banks," or they can be spaced at various intervals, depending on the size and importance of the merchandise units. An incidental benefit of removable dividers is that building costs are reduced.

3. *Height:* Many display managers could tell about their experiences with clubs. The Women's Club, the Boy Scouts, the Chamber of Commerce, and other civic groups are sometimes loaned a window by public spirited store managers. The displayman can install the

display for them or he can turn them loose to trim the window themselves. If he follows the last course, the amateur displaymen will invariably crowd about 90% of the material onto the floor. Only 10% will be off the floor. The effect from the street will be that of a nearly empty window.

This illustrates the most common failing, compositionally speaking, of beginning displaymen. It is the lack of height in display.

What are the basics of display height? Naturally, one can work up from the floor (elevation) or down from the ceiling (suspension), or a combination of the two.

Flats, panels, tables and shelves, extensible standards, flat based fixtures of all types, spring cap poles, and the mannequins themselves are the devices used to achieve elevation from the floor. For suspension from the ceiling, a grid as described in Chapter 2 is the answer. The way of actually attaching to the grid can be as varied as the display. Thin wire, nylon thread (in the same color as the background), or transparent fishing leader are good if the means of suspension are to be invisible. Ribbon, light brass chain, sisal cord, white cotton rope, or plastic chain are all good if the means of suspension can be seen.

Two words of caution about the choice of materials. *First,* if one is not very careful, the means of achieving height will dominate the display. The means should be as inconspicuous as possible unless it has a truly decorative appearance that will enhance the over-all effect. Too many wires, threads, stands, and other hardware can destroy the good appearance of a display. *Second,* chain, tie wire, etc., should be perpendicular if it is visible. The weight of the object will usually take care of this problem, but it should always be double-checked when the display is complete. The only exception to this last point might be a case in which the loose end of ribbon or whatever is draped in a decorative way, but this, as can readily be seen, does not invalidate the rule because it involves the unattached end rather than the actual suspension.

Very popular devices for achieving elevation are spring cap poles. These are sometimes wood but the most popular models are made of aluminum. Originally a display fixture, they have been adopted by interior decorators for lamps, room dividers, etc. They are very versatile with a wide variety of shelves, hooks and sign holders; they are light-weight; and, of course, their chief advantage is the ease with which they can be installed and their adaptability to any ceiling height.

A simple rule-of-thumb is used for building from the floor by experienced persons. Many display fixtures are extensible, in the manner of a telescope. If they are opened to their maximum elevation they are apt to be top heavy, both visually and actually. *Heights greater than thirty-six inches from the window floor should be obtained by using a table or shelf to support the fixture.*

4. *Angles:* Too many cooks spoil the broth and too many angles spoil a display. Too many angles make a messy, cluttered look. This is an axiom that displaymen must remember.

The rule applies if we are talking about the display seen from the front or seen from above. At least two major compositional elements should be placed parallel with the front of the display (the window glass or the front edge of a table) and at least two elements should be parallel with the "frame of reference" (window walls, the walls of a shadow box or other interior display area, or the vertical and horizontal edges of a table).

Do not be mechanical in the selection of angles, however. For example, in most windows it is best to place the "readers" parallel to the glass. From time to time a window may not look right with the "reader" placed this way. If this is the case don't hesitate to place it at an angle.

This leads to an interesting visual phenomenon. We "feel" that objects placed at an angle are moving in that direction. For this reason the elements of the display should not be placed so that they face out of the composition. Of course, if a large number of similar items make up the display, as a group of ladies' hats, for example, some may face out for the sake of variety. The ones that face out, however, should not be at the right or left margins. The items at the right and left margins will "stop" the "felt" movement if they are placed at an angle facing into the display.

Here, as in the matter of balance, the ability to recognize "felt" angles must be almost intuitive. Some time will pass before the inexperienced person can recognize the suggestion of movement that is implied by placement of objects at various angles. The inexperienced person will see the fault but won't be able to define it. He will describe it as "it just doesn't seem right" or something similar. The skilled displayman learns through experience to set it right by the judicious change of an angle or two.

It is impossible to say how many angles should be used. As a starter the apprentice should limit himself to the lines parallel to the front of the display and the "frame of reference" plus one angle. As soon as he has mastered this type of composition he can venture into more experimental arrangements. This advice may seem dogmatic but at least the novice will not offend the visual sensibilities of his customers while he is developing his own ability to handle more intricate display compositions.

COLOR AND MOTION IN DISPLAY

Color in display has several dimensions. It is the most valuable way of promoting fashion merchandise. The importance of color in this respect will be discussed in more detail in Chapter 6. Suffice it to say here that the displayman must keep constantly abreast of the latest color fashions. He can do this by studying price lists, by studying fashion forecasts, through discussion with the fashion merchandise buyers, and by reading current periodicals.

Some merchants have shown inventiveness in the choice of colors to indicate the seasons. Most follow the more or less stereotyped choices.

The actual choice is not as important (there are literally hundreds of possible choices) as restraint. The very multiplicity of choice is what creates the problem. Simplify your color scheme when the time comes to plan another season. No more than two basic colors for overall store decor in each season is advisable. Greater impact comes through repetition of the basic colors. For example, suppose pink and chartreuse are selected as basic colors for the spring period. As the customer goes from the windows to the interior she sees pink and chartreuse repeated in props, in merchandise, in every part of the store. She will know something is going on! Use only the more masculine color if one seems too feminine for the men's department. However, even pink can be used with restraint in men's wear displays if it is limited to foliage or a touch or two in the background or signs. Most displaymen recall how pink was promoted as a merchandise color in men's wear, and quite successfully at that.

Yellow, lavender and pastel blues and greens are also good spring colors. Summer colors tend more toward bold, strident tones; orange, marine blue, ochre, palm green, to name but a few. Fall colors (this includes back-to-school) are rich and usually darker tones such as red, violet, brown, gold, deep green, etc. Christmas is not always traditional red and green. Try a white Christmas for a change of pace. Gold, silver, aqua and pink are other possibilities.

To be perfectly practical about the choice of colors take a good look at the manufacturers' offerings in foliage, paper, ribbons and paints for the approaching season. It is all very well to say that a little dab of color of your own mixture will be the basic color, but if it is impossible to get foliage, seamless papers, ribbons, etc., that harmonize you are just making your job more difficult.

To describe a color we refer to its *hue,* to its *chroma or intensity,* and to its *value. Hue* is the name of the color, red, yellow, blue, etc. *Chroma* or intensity is the degree of saturation. *Value* refers to the range of grays from white through black.

Color systems have little communicative value. Displaymen should familiarize themselves with their essentials but real knowledge comes from actually working with color. We soon learn that each color system is based on a limited conception. For example, the color "wheel" will indicate the approximate color that will result from mixing adjacent hues but bears little relationship to prismatic color or that which results from the mixture of colored light.

The spread of color by a prism results because the molecular composition of the prism slows down colors as they pass through. Red travels through glass fastest, while violet is slowest compared to the others. The displayman will recognize that the mixture of prismatic color is quite different from the mixture of pigments which are either native earths or chemical dyes.

Reduction of the amount of light through a prism will result in a darker value of the original hue. One might suppose that the addition of black or white to pigment would result in a lighter or darker value of the original hue but this is usually not the case. For example, the addition of black to yellow results in a rich green instead of a dark yellow. Even the mixture of black and white pigments does not result in a true gray. The result is a bluish gray.

Many theories have been developed on color. One of the best known is the Munsell color designation system. Munsell recognized a total of 100 different hues around a wheel, starting with a basic five, yellow, red, purple, blue and green. The mixture of two adjacent hues results in an "intermediate" hue.

The Ostwald system recognizes 24 colors around a wheel. Supporters of this system argue that his basic 4 colors, yellow, red, blue, and seagreen are arranged more exactly opposite their true complements than other systems.

The Munsell and Ostwald systems differ from the well known "color wheel" for color mixing that we recall from our earliest school years. This wheel has three "primary" colors, red, yellow, and blue, and three "secondary" colors, orange, violet, and green, that result from mixing two primaries. Orange results from red and yellow, violet results from red and blue, and green results from blue and yellow.

The practical value of color "wheels" in display planning is that they are a compact reference for the selection of color combinations that provide the desired visual and psychological qualities. For example, complementary hues (those at opposite sides of the wheel) will give maximum contrast of hue while adjacent hues contrast the least.

If a three-color composition is desired, maximum contrast will be obtained by using "split complements." For example, yellow, red-violet, and blue-violet. The split comes on the violet but it could be the other way around; violet, yellow-green, and yellow-orange. To continue with the same example, a two-color complement would be yellow and violet.

Color combinations based on complementary, split complementary, and adjacent hues are considered harmonious. Harmony is not always the object in display, however. Just as modern music and art are sometimes developed around dissonant combinations, so too, some of the most striking color combinations in display and fashions occur through the deliberate manipulation of dissonance.

Incidentally, most stores receive free display materials (dealer displays) from manufacturers. Much of this material is designed without much thought about the displayman's problems, but some of it is very good. If an otherwise good dealer display cannot be used because it does not harmonize with the wall or other colors, try separating them with a broad band of white or black. Sometimes this will be enough to permit the use together of otherwise distasteful combinations. In other words, white or black can be used to build margins around color.

In the preceding paragraphs we have discussed contrast as it refers to hues on a color wheel. Contrast is also obtained by *value* control. *Value,* it will be recalled, is the range of grays from white to black. Every hue has an intrinsic value. For example, yellow has a lighter intrinsic value than blue (the same intensity or chroma is assumed). One can get a fairly clear idea of the value of a color by painting two-inch squares of yellow, orange, red, green, blue, and violet and matching them with grays mixed from black and white.

Thus, if a displayman using a composition of blue and yellow, for example, wishes to reduce contrast without changing hues he must alter the other variable. Since experience has taught him that black added to yellow pigment will result in green instead of a darker yellow, he must bring the two values closer together by adding white to the blue. Blue remains fairly close to its original hue when white or black is added so in this case a lighter blue will result instead of another color.

Chroma or intensity, the third facet of color description, is, in a way, outside the control of the displayman. It has to do with the strength of pigment or dye that has been used. It comes as a surprise to many persons to learn that all commercially prepared colors contain a large percentage of inert matter or extender, usually aluminum stearate. The cheaper the product the more extender (law requires the statement of contents on the container in most cases).

The so-called "fluorescent" paints (DayGlo is one of the trade names) are an example of very high intensity pigment. A "fluorescent" color may be the same hue and value as paint by another manufacturing process, but chroma or intensity has been raised by the use of a minimum amount of inert matter and by increasing the light reflective properties of the pigment by coarse grinding and the use of particularly reflective pigments.

Blues, greens, and violets are called *cool colors*. Yellows, oranges, and reds are called *warm* colors. Cool colors seem to recede in space as contrasted with warm colors which seem to advance. This information is important to displaymen because it aids them in the creation of an illusion of depth. Two objects on the same plane will appear to advance or recede, dependent on the color choice.

Warm and cool colors enhance the actual temperature. The yellows, oranges, and reds appear hot. Too much hot color in a window facing a street where passersby are sweltering in 110 degree temperatures would not have the desired impact to say the least.

Some colors fade faster than others when exposed to sunlight. Careful merchandise placement and frequent changes can cut this kind of markdown to a minimum. The most fugitive (fastest fading) colors are varieties of blue. A little different problem, but quite alarming the first time it happens to an apprentice displayman, is the effect of a hot iron on red fabrics. Most red fabrics will darken under a hot iron but the original color will return as the fabric cools.

Aside from color mixing, there is another quite different aspect of color in display. This has to do with the complexities of symbolism. This always relates to our culture and is consequently subject to the vagaries of time and place. A color symbol in the United States may have a very different meaning in another part of the world. For example, red can mean sin, danger, or anger. And in recent years it has become the symbolic color of the communist part of the world.

A few of the other important meanings that we assign to colors are: purple for royalty, pink for femininity, white for purity, black for death, blue for aristocracy, and so on. The displayman must learn to recognize these assigned color meanings and use them to express ideas in display. At the same time he must be careful not to offend the customer with distasteful symbolism. For example, the thoughtless use of black as a border might suggest mourning instead of standing as an abstract element of the design.

Motion in display can mean the wide assortment of turntables, electric motors, fans and other novelties to actually make things move. It can mean graphic devices to suggest motion, or it can mean the multiple points of view assumed by the spectator as she passes the display, either on foot or in an automobile. Let us list a few of the reasons for using motion in display and the techniques involved:

1. Motion to display more than one side of an object. If an item can be sold more easily by showing several sides a motion device should be considered. What items lend themselves to this? Any clothing that has an interesting detail on the back, furniture, appliances, automobiles and boats are but a few.

2. Motion is used to attract the eye to the merchandise. Props suspended from electric motors, built up from turntables, and activated by fans can, if properly used, catch the eye and direct it to the merchandise. A large number of dealer displays are made today that are activated by flashlight batteries. Some are excellent. One or two that come to mind immediately as good examples are a replica of the Seattle world's fair tower with a rotating top that would have fit perfectly into travel windows at that time, or a wheel that rotates slowly to show the wide range of prints available in a fabric to match a solid color in the same fabric. Both ideas were simple, they were in good taste, and they were merchandise oriented.

3. Motion suggested in backgrounds. Very stylish display props can be made by borrowing a trick from the art movements, such as futurism, cubism, "pop," or "op." These artists are very interested in the dynamics of modern life and try to depict this dynamism through multiple images, foggy outlines and other identifiable techniques. For display purposes the design can be either painted or drawn on a background or created by multiple exposure with a camera or oscilloscope.

Devices for creating motion in display should be used with restraint. The final judgment of whether to use motion or not must not be based on the novelty of the idea but on its potential for creating sales. Failure to follow this rule will result in distraction of the customer from the sales message and a cheap effect.

"There's double excitement in Bonwit's B. H. Wragge Room — a new exhibit of contemporary art, and a new collection of resort things. Fifth Floor

chapter 6

development of ideas

W HERE do we get ideas for displays? As we think this question through make notes about its application to your own store. It is extremely important for every display manager and store owner to understand his policy better by putting it in written form.

6
7

The American consumer has been conditioned by sales messages. She is surrounded and bombarded with newspaper ads, radio and TV commercials, billboards, circulars, sky-writers, magazine ads, point-of-purchase display and windows. As a result, she is apt not to notice much of it at all. The merchant with the only chance of getting through is the fellow who knows how to build displays that compel attention.

The cardinal rule for compelling attention is simplicity. *It means selling one idea at a time.* It means thinking carefully about the idea you want to communicate and eliminating everything that confuses that idea. Please note that this does not necessarily mean eliminating large amounts of merchandise. It does mean simplification and clarification of the idea. The idea should be so clear that it can be incorporated in a caption of four or five words that will be used on the lead line of the sign or "reader." This caption is sometimes referred to as "key copy." If the item is advertised in the newspaper or magazines the "key copy" should be repeated.

Maybe you are saying to yourself "This argument for simplicity is nice, but I doubt if I'll get everything I want to show into the display this way." For the doubting Thomases, think what a project it is to trim the average assortment type window. It usually means staying late and bending and squatting in cramped quarters until your muscles ache. Couldn't you change windows with hard-sell ideas more often? In the long run, as much if not more will be displayed, and with more sales appeal!

Recent studies on impulse buying point up the effectiveness of hard-hitting sales messages. The survey of Drug Store Brand Switching and Impulse Buying made by the Point-of-Purchase Advertising Institute shows that "Display generated three out of ten impulse sales, three out of ten in-store brand switches (five out of six of which occurred in impulse purchases) and three out of ten specific brand selections where brand was not important to the customer. In addition, it should be remembered that many purchases made by the interviewed customers were attributed by the customer to the fact that the item was on sale. This was true in some cases, but in others the item was not actually on sale, but *only on special display*. The customer merely *felt* that it was on sale because of the excitement generated by the display. When it is borne in mind that over 40 per cent of the purchase decisions were made *in the store*, the importance of the role of signs and displays becomes even more evident."

Ideas for displays are as various as your imagination. However, they will usually fall into one of the categories that we will outline. These are: Color, Price, Style, Fabric, Process and Brand.

IDEAS FROM COLOR

Sure-fire traffic-stoppers are displays planned around a *COLOR*. Color promotions are seen often in dress shops. This manual is not for clothing stores alone so here are a few other color promotions:

A paint store could display a new color for home decoration. Cover a piece of wallboard with the color as a background. Leave the edges uneven. Tack the roller to the board as though the job is still in progress. Finish the display with neat stacks of cans and the color name prominently displayed on a sign.

Most of us are too modest about our creative capacities. If we don't see a new color name in a nationally distributed magazine we give up.

Take an old favorite and give it a new name! That's probably what the people working in a New York agency did. The more imaginative or "far-out" the name, the more your customers will love it. This is also an opportunity to invent color names with local appeal; New Rochelle Rose, San Mateo Mint, etc. Bringing in the home town name always creates interest.

How many people know optometrists sell colored contact lenses? Here's a color idea, and in one of the professions that has been badly neglected by free-lance displaymen! Another area that is badly neglected is banks and savings and loan associations. A bank might build a color promotion around the caption "Decorate with *green,* our favorite color!" the idea being, of course, to borrow the money and let a professional do the decorating.

White, for display purposes, is a color. Lots of shops can have "White Sales." Shirts and blouses, stationery, or candy are just three possibilities. Incidentally, the majority of sheets and household linens are still bought during "White Sales." If the idea became established with other merchandise lines it would probably be a real sales stimulant.

Another idea is to use color only in accessories. For example, the neckties in a men's window might all be shades of one color. Or, try one color for all the price tickets in a display. Repeating one color in either accessories or price tickets has several effects. First, it compels attention. Second, it unifies the display, and third, it helps, through the choice of an appropriate color, to identify the season.

IDEAS FROM PRICE

A second category for developing display ideas is *PRICE*. Of course, merchandise for this kind of display must have inherent price appeal. This type of window is often used in months when it is a little more difficult to get people into the store. Merchandise of this type is sometimes called "loss leaders" or "traffic items" or "hot shots."

One word of caution about this kind of idea. You may develop great skill in trimming, but it is usually very difficult to make cheap merchandise look better than it really is (an exception might be truly quality merchandise that has been marked down because of inventory or related problems). Because its deficiencies are readily apparent, use merchandise specially purchased for price promotions with caution. Most of the time, try to put your best foot forward in window displays. At the point-of-purchase leave "hot-shot" merchandise folded. Make the sign with the price the biggest element of the display. The big blast on "hot-shots" should be in newspaper advertising where a half-tone illustration won't reveal its shortcomings.

A *PRICE* idea permits you to get a large number of items in the window. An example that comes immediately to mind are 88¢ toy or tool displays. These have been "beaten to death," of course, but you can think of some fresh ideas for your store. Note that the unusual number 88 contributes to the attention compelling possibilities of this kind of window.

In connection with price ideas, it should be pointed out that most merchants use "comparative prices." An example is "this item was $1.98 . . . now only $1." This is certainly an effective selling tool. It has been abused in some cases, however. Some stores prohibit the use of comparative prices as a matter of policy, their argument being that it is possible for an unethical merchant to mark something up just so it can be marked down again.

Proper signing is possibly more important with *PRICE* promotions than with any other category. Make your price windows as heavy or light as you please, but don't forget to let the passersby know what's going on with a sign that really shouts the featured price!

Let us mention here two special events that should be in the idea repertoire of every displayman. They are essentially price ideas. One is the End-of-Month Cleanup. The other is Dollar Days. EOM can be scheduled every month or only occasionally as the store inventory demands. It is designed to move out-of-season merchandise, discontinued items, soiled and damaged merchandise, and bad buys.

Dollar Days is a tradition in many stores that is eagerly anticipated by regular customers. Merchandise is specially purchased or is marked down just for the period of the promotion. Not every item on display has to be sold at a dollar figure. However, with a little preparation, the majority of lead items can be priced at dollar figures. For example, a regular 49¢ item would probably sell as well at 2 for $1. Two Dollar Days events each year are scheduled in many locations.

IDEAS FROM STYLE

A third category for developing display ideas is *STYLE*. We know from sales results that style really moves merchandise. People are keenly interested in innovation. Price will attract women much of the time but it had better be a real bargain! American women are too astute to be fooled very often. What most really want is to live like the prototypes they see in Ladies' Home Journal ads.

Don't think style promotions are limited to ladies' ready-to-wear. Many other examples can be brought to mind. Foundation garments to wear with sportswear would be a good idea for a lingerie shop. How about a new stroller design for a lead item in the infant's department? Contrast it with one of the older models, the way the auto dealers do.

Fig. 48

Fig. 49

Fig. 51

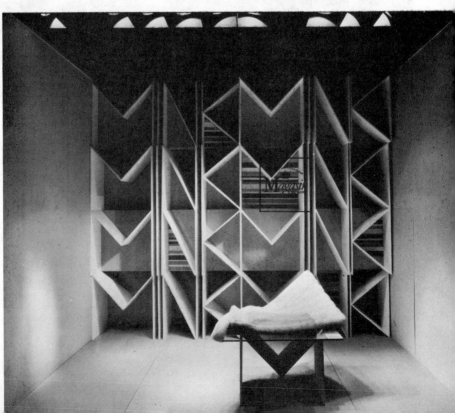

A new cut in jackets, a lining, or a new collar are all promotable items in men's wear. Furniture manufacturers are constantly rediscovering the beauty of a *period*. The past masters of style promotion are, of course, the automobile industry. For several years new mechanical ideas were at a virtual standstill but high volume was maintained by style promotion.

IDEAS FROM PROCESS, FABRIC, BRAND

COLOR, PRICE, or *STYLE* then, will be the idea mainstays for most displaymen. Other ideas can be built around a *PROCESS* (A process idea might include two appliances, one assembled and one partially dis-assembled. The parts of the dis-assembled unit would be labeled to show their function.), a *FABRIC* (A fabric idea could simply be an assortment of garments made with the featured fabric or it might show the finished product and samples of the raw material. Or, it might contrast the virtues of the featured fabric with another fabric.), or a *BRAND* (A brand idea would, of course, feature the brand name perhaps with additional signs pointing out the product's virtues).

This method of developing ideas has been called *Item Promotion*. It is based on well-founded psychological principles. The human mind has limited retentive powers. Display will have a better chance of making its point, of being remembered if it expresses one major idea at a time. The old idea of putting one of everything in the window and hoping for the best has been proven fallacious.

Three general rules about the development of ideas may be helpful:

• Rule number 1: *Seasonal backgrounds and item promotions are not mutually exclusive.* A seasonal background can remain intact while three or four item promotions are changed in front of it (Chapter 7 will show how displaymen can save a lot of time by adapting displays). Let us suppose, just as one example, that an item promotion in the holiday season is pink sleepwear. The season is holiday and the item promotion is the color "pink." The next week might still be holiday season but the item promotion for the week might be style or any of the other item ideas.

How much seasonal and item ideas overlap will depend on the item, the season, the time available for building new displays, and budget, just to name some of the most important factors.

Incidentally, "season" in display work is a somewhat ambiguous term. We build the basic color plan around the four major seasons of the year, Spring, Summer, Fall and Winter. Beyond this, most retail establishments elaborate on "season" with the more accurate term "special event." The following are listed as a guide to some of the most important:

Spring: Washington's Birthday, Valentine's Day, St. Patrick's Day, Easter.

Summer: Mother's Day, Memorial Day, Father's Day, 4th of July.

Fall: Back-to-School, Hallowe'en, Thanksgiving.

Winter: Holiday, Winter Cruise, White Goods.

Anniversary, Birthday and Clearance events are worked into the Special Events schedule according to the store's tradition and policy.

• Rule number 2: *Keep the merchandise the most important part of the idea.* The merchandise is, after all, the reason for the display. Pick it up, compare it, study it, talk about it, understand its good and bad points before developing any display ideas. This may sound very obvious but it is amazing how many times merchandise has been forced to fit an idea instead of the other way around.

• Rule number 3: *Give the idea a "handle" early in the planning process.* This will usually be the caption or key copy mentioned earlier. By deciding on a caption before a lot of work has been done, all participants in the venture, displayman, merchant, advertising department, sign writers, and so on, are talking a common language. It identifies the nature of the promotion. Everyone knows what he is trying to accomplish.

There should never be an excuse for a displayman to say "I don't have an idea"! In addition to *Color, Price, Style, Fabric, Process,* and *Brand* promotions, interspersed and reinforced with special events, every displayman should keep *party themes* in his bag of tricks.

You will realize, upon reflection, that a Valentine party and a Christmas party might contain almost identical merchandise. The only difference would be a cupid and bow prop instead of a Christmas tree. This illustrates the versatility of the party theme as a year-round display idea. Even the gift-wrapped boxes (empty of course) could conceivably be utilized again.

Have a birthday party or invent your own party theme if there isn't a major holiday in the month. Confetti and favors purchased in the five and dime may be the only cost for props. Try swim or slumber parties for eye-catching changes of pace if the merchandise seems to fit. Party themes, as is true of all selling displays, should feature a color, a price, a style, or some other item idea.

Wit in display is a very important ingredient. Many stories could be told about the outstanding success of promotional ideas that caricature our buying habits in a good-natured way. The application of wit in display is sometimes similar to the "funny paper" style used in advertising. More often it is more subtle, by the association of incongruous things, by the introduction of the unexpected, and by exaggeration of forms that have a new meaning when seen out of scale.

There is a delicate balance point where wit in display becomes offensive. Instead of being amused, the shopper may be insulted by your efforts. Certain limits must be recognized. An example may help to understand this point.

A neatly dressed mannequin was posed in a Dollar Day window to look like a shopper almost smothered in bargains. Customers were amused by the slight exaggeration of the "shopper's" disarray and confusion. In another store the identical situation was used but the mannequin was posed in an unflattering way, and in general, made to look like a fool. The gross mishandling of the idea repelled women instead of attracting them.

Men don't seem to be as easily offended by wit in display as women. One can use "corny" ideas in men's windows. The omission of trousers on men mannequins, mannequin heads placed to look like an accident, etc., can even be used occasionally. Put your sales messages on cardboard cut to look like "funny paper" balloons. Hang them with transparent thread. The all-important thing is to remember not to overdo the "corn" and be certain that it really contributes something to the promotion.

No manual on display would really be complete without brief mention of two time-worn favorites, one a "spectacular," the other pure "corn."

Cut a brick in two, glue half to either side of the window to make it appear that it was thrown through the glass, paint jagged lines radiating from the brick, and letter on the glass . . . (you guessed it) "Prices Smashed" or something similar.

The other is called the "Invisible Fish Trick." Place a goldfish bowl, complete with water, rocks, and all the accessories except the fish in the window. Place a neatly lettered card alongside with "This bowl contains an invisible Hawaiian Leopardfish!" Believe it or not, people will crane their necks trying to see it! The merchandise tie-in is more difficult in this case but should not be ignored. Try another card that says "Our bargains are recognized by everyone."

Brief mention was made in Chapter 4 of the need to show the "end use" of merchandise. This should be part of every display, cutting through item, seasonal, special event, or other ideas. In her final judgment your customer will buy only if she can visualize the merchandise as part of her life. Helping her with this visualization is the meaning of "end use" demonstration.

A candid display manager will tell you that there is very little in his business that is truly original. We all strive to add a completely unique idea to the display scene but the day-in, day-out job is done by the adaptation of favorite ideas, with a new twist here and there, by borrowing (a polite term) what has been seen in competitive stores, and by the gradual improvement of time-tested techniques. This leads up to a very important suggestion. Every display department should keep an Idea File.

Some stores categorize their Idea File by seasons. Others do so by color, price, style, and so on. The breakdown that works best for your store should be used, naturally. Two or three loose leaf binders are ample in many cases. Others may want to use filing cabinets. Snapshots, newspaper clippings, magazine ads, sketches of competition windows are a few of the things that can go into the file.

It is very well to understand the importance of item promotion, to know how to handle merchandise flawlessly, and to know how to organize one's work, but the display idea must still be put into a specific form. This is where the somewhat intangible role of imagination takes over. The question then follows "Can the displayman's imagination be developed, and if so, how?"

The answer is an emphatic yes, imagination can be developed. The best displaymen are keen students of their fellowmen. The displayman's best stimulant to the imagination are the dreams and aspirations of his customers. He draws from every kind of experience.

A style idea may take the form of a current event or headline. A color idea might tie-in with a hue of popular interest in an entirely different field, gardening for example. Most displaymen are very interested in the other art forms, drama, painting, music, sculpture, and so on. Music and literature have inspired many beautiful displays. The modern interest in space travel has given rise to innumerable display ideas.

Our displayman must be an expert in matters of public taste. He must be able to show his customers that the store he works for can fulfill their dreams of a richer life. Stand in front of a really good window and you will feel that the displayman felt a deep sympathy and understanding for the shopper. If the beginning displayman can learn to develop that kind of feeling, he will never have to worry about a lack of ideas.

chapter 7

time organization—
routine and beyond

A CTUAL practice varies widely from store to store, but the following outline will give an idea of the way promotions are planned:

1. From four to six months in advance, the promotional plan is tentatively set. The general guide in all promotional planning must, of course, be past experience. If a February Dollar Days, for example, was a whopping success last year it will probably be scheduled again this year. If it was not successful something else will be planned. Planning at this stage is not very specific. The theme is set, the overall goals and budget are discussed, and responsibilities assigned. The buyers will be told the general types of merchandise to be selected. The Display Manager and Advertising Manager will confer to insure the closest possible coordination.

2. From two to three months in advance of the promotion orders are placed with manufacturers. The Display Manager receives a list of specific items and window and point-of-purchase assignments are made. The Display Manager will complete plans for item promotions at this time, including orders for any props that were not included in the seasonal plan (Seasonal display planning must be done further in advance, usually four to six months).

3. Three weeks in advance of the promotion the Display Manager will give the buyer a requisition for display merchandise. The requisition will be for specific items needed for windows and point-of-purchase displays. The requisition should specify quantities, colors, and sizes. Merchandise that must be pressed will be turned in to the tailor shop. That which does not require pressing can be turned in to the display shop, held in the stock room, or whatever seems most appropriate.

This should be the final date for major merchandise substitution. If the buyer wishes to make a substitution he should notify the Display Manager and get his okay. The very complicated job of organizing promotions will not permit last-minute changes except for the most imperative reasons (merchandise not delivered, an abrupt and decisive style change makes the merchandise unsalable, etc.).

An important part of the requisition should be a space for sign copy. This point has been warmly debated. Some say that the display department or the ad department should write copy. It is the author's contention that the merchant should be responsible. He knows the good and bad points of the item (he bought it, after all); therefore, he is the one best prepared to describe it. The Display Manager should be able to recommend phrasing that will bring copy into closer alignment with the promotional idea, but the final responsibility must be with the buyer.

4. Four days in advance of the promotion the Display Manager makes a final check of all details of the plan, including merchandise pulled and pressed, backgrounds and props prepared insofar as possible, and signs and readers ready.

Most clothing cannot be pressed further in advance than four days because it will be crushed if left on a rack in the tailor shop or hanger marks will develop. Any merchandise that can be put on forms in the display shop should be done at this time.

5. Display installation day should include a check of the finished work by the Display Manager and the buyer together.

6. The display is "pulled" after a specified period (one week is common practice with most store windows), and a record is made of its effectiveness.

If one realizes that the above outline is multiplied in an average sized department store by several such promotions every day, each working day of the week, it is easy to see how much careful coordination is necessary between the merchandising and sales promotion departments.

There must be flexibility in the plan. Merchandise may be delayed; displays must be "pulled" sooner than anticipated, and so on. The plan must be practical. Our hypothetical Display Manager may know how to "handle" specific lines of merchandise, how to compose displays, how to find ideas, but if he can't find enough hours in a day to get it done all else will have been in vain. The adaptation of these principles to large or small operations will not invalidate them.

Several general principles should be followed for individual work scheduling whether the shop is a one-man operation or a giant department store:

1. Every displayman should set aside one full day each week for preparation. This proposal will astound many experienced displaymen. Stores willing to give the idea an honest trial will find that one full day out of the windows or off the selling floor for the supervision of merchandise selection, grooming of merchandise, preparation of props and backgrounds, and vital paperwork will actually save time and result in better displays. The displayman who never allows time for preparation is always behind and his work will look rushed.

2. Laymen (we'll include store managers in this category) don't always understand the deadlines in display work. Display space is the most valuable square footage in the store. It costs the store money to let it stand idle. Most displaymen realize this and will stay late to finish rather than leave a display incomplete.

Unfortunately, a few managers exploit the conscientious character of their Display Manager. Rather than seek a solution to the problem of late hours this type of manager is quite happy to let the display department continue to work unnecessarily long hours.

Here are several specific, time-tested ways to organize time:

a. A regularly scheduled preparation day mentioned earlier.

b. Overtime or compensatory time off if a display can't be completed in a normal work day. This has the added advantage of permitting changes after hours or other than peak traffic hours.

c. Trimming in banks mentioned in Chapter 5. Repetition of props and setup can save much time.

d. In larger stores, more of the display staff can be "ganged-up" on a single project. Space limitations must be considered carefully before doing this, however. Too many persons working in a small area may delay the work.

e. Finally, the most important single trick, if we can call it that, is to think of every display by elements, as mentioned in Chapter 5. Recall that almost all displays have the following elements: Background, setup, major and minor merchandise units, accessories, floor covering or base, and reader and price tickets.

Let us assume, as an example, that it takes from 8 a.m. until 5 p.m. for our displayman to finish the first three elements in a display, i.e., background, setup, major and minor merchandise units. Let's also assume he prepared properly, that extra help was not available, and that overtime pay was ruled out by the "front office."

If he has completed the first three elements he can leave until the next day provided he makes a careful check to see that the lights are on, that all tools, etc., have been removed from the display site, and that the store manager has been notified of his intentions.

In other words, a display minus accessories, floor covering, and reader and price tickets can be left overnight. It will not be as rich or inform the shopper as well as it might, but it will be neat and appear finished. In recommending this "trick" however, it should be emphasized that it is only a last resort, it is not a substitute for careful planning, and the incomplete display must be neat, no tools left on the floor, no loose pins or staples, etc. The slightest mess will give the whole thing away.

3. Displaymen should allow a "cushion" in every working day for unforeseen situations. This, of course, does not mean that the time will be wasted if the unforeseen situation does not materialize. Displays must be "pulled" because the merchandise is sold out. Perhaps the manager wants to discuss something that he thinks needs immediate attention (it might wait but not many will tell him so).

"Try-ons" are another problem. Many can be deferred by the application of a consistent policy. The sales person can tell the customer that her name will be pinned to the back of the garment. She will have first chance to purchase when the display is removed. Give her a specific date. If she insists, and most won't if the policy is politely explained, the display department should be called and the "try-on" cheerfully made.

With the possible exception of the most exclusive specialty shops, good planning will eliminate the need for most "try-ons." The merchandise should really not be on display if there is none to sell. But even in the best managed stores these situations will occasionally arise. It is better to have a policy and plan the time necessary for the implementation of the policy than to have everyone thrown into utter consternation every time an unexpected situation arises. Thus the reason for the "cushion" in each displayman's daily schedule.

In connection with "try-ons" it should be mentioned that hardly anything will spoil the appearance of a store so quickly as bare fixtures. If merchandise is sold and cannot be immediately replaced, be certain that the fixture is returned to the fixture storage area.

Rotation: This is a vital part of display routine. While the job is done mostly by sales personnel the displayman must exert some control over this important activity. Glass and miscellaneous fixture hardware used in rotation is stored in or near the display shop. The displayman must insist that sales people police this area themselves. If it is not kept orderly the work will suffer.

Rotation is the systematic movement of merchandise from favored positions to less favored positions, dependent on its timeliness and its profit potential. The productivity of certain display areas can be proven beyond any doubt. Sales of a slow moving item will pick up if placed in another position. The authoritative study made by the Point-of-Purchase Advertising Institute showed that "Per linear foot, by dollars, the relative merchandising productivity of displays is twelve to one as against normal shelf positions."

Aside from the increased sales of specific items that results, rotation gives the store an ever new and fresh look that will bring regular customers back again and again.

Full Shelves: Underlying all display routine must be an understanding of the interesting psychological phenomenon involved in the amount of merchandise visible. Half empty, poorly arranged shelves do not excite as much interest as stocky but neat arrangements. Well stocked shelves give the impression of something going on, of a sale. On the other hand blank spaces give the impression that the store is poorly managed or "out of business."

Of course, the principle of full shelves will be more important to self-service and open stock stores than to specialty shops featuring personal service. It all depends on the image the store desires to build. In the last instance quality and status values are enhanced by keeping a lot of merchandise out of sight or in show cases.

Related Items: Reference was made briefly to related items in an earlier chapter. This important phase of display is discussed again here because thinking in terms of related items should become routine.

A related item is merchandise that is related in terms of function; slippers with sleepwear, neckties with shirts, beach towels with swimwear, and so on.

Related item selling and its concomitant function, related item display, are among the most powerful selling tools at your command. It boils down to selling an entire package. If a lady buys a coat she will probably want new shoes to go with it. Show her how much nicer the coat will look with a new hat, and who ever wears shoes with a handbag that doesn't match?

Related item thinking should become routine. It applies to every retail field. Here again the automobile industry has developed this kind of selling to its n'th degree. What a difference there is between the "stripped" and the fully equipped models! The extra chrome is a related item just as much as the hat is to the lady's coat.

MORE ASPECTS OF DISPLAY ROUTINE (Two Time Savers)

Most displays can be adapted to accommodate more than one kind of merchandise. Let us say, for example, that the window schedule as originally planned for the men's windows in the first week of the spring period are those shown in the left hand column. The second week schedule is shown in the second column:

	1st Week	2nd Week
Window 1:	dress shirts	swimwear
Window 2:	sport coats/slacks	sport shirts
Window 3:	underwear	suits

By taking a moment or two to study this list the alert display manager can save himself hours of work simply by revising the list as follows:

Window 1:	dress shirts	sport shirts
Window 2:	sport coats/slacks	suits
Window 3:	underwear	swimwear

All he has done to schedule the windows so that he can use the setup for two weeks instead of one. This is possible because fixtures are able to wear more than one line. In this example, the same shirt forms can be used for dress or sport shirts, the same suit forms can be used for suits or sport coats, and the same forms can be used for underwear or swimwear.

Adapting displays is certainly a time-saver. However, it should always be done with care. All other factors must be equal before adaptation can be successful. For example, the dress shirt window in the example may require a seasonal background while the sport shirt window needs a strictly "item" approach. If this is so, the job may as well be started from scratch. Also, the kind of window will have a bearing on the decision to adapt or start with a new setup. One window may be a "straight" type in an important traffic location. If the original schedule is altered an item that needs exposure to traffic may be moved to an "L" or some other shape window. In every case that the schedule is altered the displayman must notify the department heads and explain his reasoning.

A second routine time-saver has been discussed in terms of composition. This is trimming either windows or interior displays in "banks." Let's take another example. If two persons are working on a "bank" of four or five windows, the work can be divided in a very mechanical way. The journeyman may complete any forming that is necessary in the shop while his helper or apprentice is "pulling" the old windows, vacuuming the floors, and replacing burned-out lights.

After the old windows are pulled, the journeyman will probably start to assemble backgrounds while the helper assembles fixtures. Wherever possible one person works from right to left while the other works from left to right. In this way they do not interfere with one another in the restricted space.

On the next sequence one person may complete the assembly of backgrounds while the other completes the setups. Then one may dress the mannequins while the other takes care of the floor coverings. Finally, one person can add the accessory units while the other places readers, price tickets and adjusts the lights.

Working from opposite ends of the "bank" also gives a uniformity to the trim that would not result if two persons worked on the same display at once. The finished windows will have a continuity that is very eye-appealing.

The finished result does not need to look mechanical. Little variations are made as the work progresses; the slight change of an angle here, a gesture of the mannequin, and so on. This will give an effect of richness and variety within a compositional unity. The general method described can be used for interior displays as well as for windows.

The experienced displayman knows the value of working from a cart. Lightweight aluminum carts are available in many designs. They can be supplemented with drawers and shelves to fit each display department's needs. Instead of making many trips back and forth between the display and the display shop, learn to load as much as possible on the cart. Park it in a light traffic area near the display site. Many steps will be saved by developing this habit.

PRESTIGE AND INSTITUTIONAL DISPLAYS

Every store is approached many times each year by civic and philanthropic groups for displays. These and the displays that depict an aspect of store policy are called prestige displays. They can be sub-divided further into these classifications:

1. Institutional Displays: These are most often in conjunction with anniversary events. They deal with an aspect of the store's history, its policies, its place in the community, and so on. Anniversary events are an opportunity to bring everyone in the store into the act. Clerks can dress in old-fashioned costumes, antiques can be borrowed for display throughout the store, etc. These may also be occasions when a display would help spread the news of credit terms, layaway, new store hours, etc.

2. Civic Displays: Civic anniversaries; school events, dances, graduation; club displays such as Rotary, women's club, etc.; public works; manufacturer's displays; and civic holidays and celebrations are included in this category. Every community romanticizes its history. A clever display manager can get lots of mileage out of this kind of promotion by inviting the participation of community organizations that are, incidentally, made up of potential customers.

3. Patriotic Displays: National holidays and the dramatization of historic events of importance, for example, the first manned orbit of the earth, or the anniversary of a famous military event, are called patriotic displays.

A powerful and tasteful patriotic display can be built by any department store with a yardage department by dropping lengths of red, white, and blue percale over the front wall of the building. The vertical lengths of yardage can be weighted with 1 by 2 boards or attached to an awning with wire. This display is more eye-catching and less expensive than many manufactured displays. The only federal law concerning the display of the flag says it cannot be shown with any trademark. It must be protected from soiling and no emblem can be placed above or upon it. When displayed in the company of flags of other nations, the U.S. flag should have the place of prominence and be raised higher than the others. There are other rules of protocol with which a displayman should be aware.

4. Feature Displays: Events of popular interest, sometimes related to a famous personality of television or the movies, make good feature displays. Another idea that has been used with great effectiveness is a contrast of work and leisure activities.

5. Holiday Displays: Treatments that are not predominantly merchandising presentations come under this category. Animated displays of all kinds, Santa's workshop, musicland, candy store, and a host of other themes lend themselves to treatments usually for Christmas and

Fig. 52

Fig. 53

Fig. 54

Fig. 55

Spring-Easter. These displays, consisting of papier mache or molded plastic or rubber figures and concealed motors are quite expensive. The Silvestri Art Manufacturing Co. of Chicago is one company that specializes in their manufacture. It is common practice for many stores to recover part of the original cost by selling them after one year. In a few cases it is desirable to repeat the same display for several seasons. Less expensive non-animated holiday displays are scheduled for other occasions.

6. Opening Displays: Two major opening events are scheduled each year by most stores, Spring Opening and Fall Opening. Style should be paramount. Every possible device should be used to build suspense. Teaser ads, masked-out windows, etc., help to create suspense. Opening events are excellent times for fashion shows.

7. Prize Displays: Many local prizes are offered for excellence in display work, while national contests are conducted every year by national advertisers and manufacturers in an effort to stimulate the sale of their goods. Participation in these contests will naturally depend on the event's importance to the store, the limitations of the display budget, and the space available. It should be remembered that aside from the direct rewards for participation in contests there is a tremendous prestige value accruing to the winners.

FASHION SHOWS, FLOATS, AND EXHIBIT BOOTHS

The basic principles in construction of fashion shows, floats, and exhibit booths do not differ radically from other displays. Because of the setting, however, the practical problems will be more complicated. The provision for exits and platforms is very important in fashion shows. Fixtures that are not designed to carry much weight may be broken if the model decides to stand on it, resulting in a most humiliating experience for all. The necessity to anchor things securely to a moving platform is a practical consideration in planning floats; failure to do so could lead to disaster.

Since the emphasis throughout this manual has been on smaller shops and what might be called family-type stores, we will suggest a few ideas that may be particularly helpful to those types.

One does not need a big budget or professional models for a successful fashion show. Salesgirls, home economics students from a local high school or university, children of store personnel and members of various women's and garden clubs are a few of the sources that have been used with tremendous success.

Shows for merchandise other than ladies ready-to-wear offer another approach. A yardage promotion featuring dresses made from fabrics on display, ski clothing, and swimwear are only a suggestion of the many lines for exciting fashion shows.

Fashion shows presented on an interior stage usually have a bi-symmetrical arrangement. This makes the exit and entry easier and tends to concentrate attention on the models.

The least expensive way to make a platform for a fashion show is to push merchandise tables together. They can be covered quickly with grass mats or carpeting. It is necessary to construct sturdy portable steps to get on and off the platform. These should be saved for repeat use. The height of a graceful step is no more than four inches. Of course, no expense is involved in still another type of show in which the models simply mingle with the customers. If this type of show is planned the model must be carefully cued for the questions she will get from interested shoppers.

Another eye-catching fashion show can be staged in a window. The window can be planned so that the background will serve for the regular display as well as the fashion show. Naturally, window shows must be planned with extra attention to the matter of entrances and exits.

Three basic ways are used for commentary. The first is oral, either impromptu descriptions of the garments as the model moves back and forth, or read from a script. The second method is to turn cards on an easel. This is usually the method for window shows. The description is written on a show card. The cards are turned as the models appear, either by someone designated for this task or by the model herself. The third basic way is to combine cards with oral commentary. It is helpful to have unobtrusive music in the background in each case. A public address system for the commentator tends to be overbearing and harsh unless the room is unusually large.

Invitations and refreshments for fashion shows are not entirely a display function. They are not even mandatory in many cases. Where they are used, the display department should be brought into the planning. Responsibility for each phase of the show must be clearly assigned to prevent embarrassing slips at the last moment.

Some very exciting things are being done in the exhibit booth line with modular construction. Sections of the framework are offered in standard sizes so that booths can be quickly assembled to accommodate many lines of merchandise in many arrangements. In some cases clips are provided on the back of the frame so that pegboard, wallboard, or other insert panels can be quickly installed without the use of a hammer and nails. In fact, the most modern aluminum exhibit booth designs built on the modular principle require no tools at all for assembly. This is, of course, more important for this type of display than for

Prize-winning exhibit for American Standard uses elegant columns to tell its story.

windows or more conventional interiors because booths must be assembled and disassembled quickly and usually in areas that are quite devoid of any kind of starting point for the construction. For example, booths are sometimes constructed on the sidewalk. There isn't a wall to build from, the sidewalk is of little help, so the booth must be constructed as an integral unit. Modern designers of exhibit booth ideas have attempted to make the displayman's job as easy as possible.

A float usually starts with a wire mesh construction on the truck or trailer chassis. This is filled in with plastic or plaster of paris construction. The forms are built up using the combination of wire mesh, burlap, and plaster and completed with foliage, grass mats, etc. This rather specialized field of display that has been used more for civic type displays in the past has tremendous potentials for forward-looking displaymen in the retail field.

chapter 8

sign and price ticket policy

S IGN and pricing policy must not be a haphazard matter. It must be carefully coordinated with over-all store policy.

Pricing makes self-selection easier. Only the most exclusive specialty shops find that a policy of no prices on merchandise creates the image that they desire.

A few general considerations on pricing may be helpful:

1. If the merchandise in a group is all one price, one ticket is sufficient.

2. Price tickets should be placed flat on the merchandise and face the glass squarely wherever possible. Ticket "bugs" or plastic holders are much better than pins to hold tickets. Pins can come loose or can damage the card in an unsightly way.

3. Develop a uniform system for price-ticketing. For example, the mannequins could always be ticketed on the right shoulder. Or, they

could always be priced with a card on the base. The exact place is not as important as having a system.

4. If accessories are priced, a neater effect can be achieved by putting the prices for the entire group on one card instead of a separate ticket on each item.

More opening nights, more self-service, federal minimum wage laws, and discount type operations have all combined to make good signing more important than ever. New sign techniques are taking over more and more of the "silent salesman" job. These include illuminated signs incorporating flasher units, automatic dimmers and brighteners, sequence timers, and other attention-compelling devices. Motion will become more prevalent in signing. Signs that vary from the standard rectangular shapes have proven very successful. New inks (fluorescent, perfumed, metallic, etc.) are being introduced.

SILK SCREEN PRINTING

More detailed instruction about silk-screen printing is available in books such as "Screen Process Printing" by Albert Kosloff or in numerous articles in *Screen Process* magazine. For purposes of this manual a basic description of this important display sign method must suffice.

Silk screen printing (serigraphy, as the artists prefer to call it) is basically a stencil method. A rubber scraper mounted in a wooden handle (squeegee) forces semi-fluid inks through openings in a stencil adhered to a silk screen to make the print. The silk is attached to a sturdy wooden frame and the frame is usually hinged to a base-board.

Silk screen designs can be printed on a large variety of materials. In addition to paper and cardboard, this printing method is used on metal, plastic, cloth, or wood.

The stencil may be made in many ways. The most simple is to letter directly on the silk with a sable brush, using either show-card paint or a special block-out solution. The dried paint in the silk forms the stencil. The screen should be held up to the light after it dries so that any pinholes can be filled. If the print is made on white paper, the finished sign will consist of white letters on a colored background, the background being the part that was printed.

Slightly more complicated is a stencil made with tracing paper. The first stroke of the squeegee (a rubber strip on a wooden handle, used to force the ink through the pores of the silk) causes the ink to adhere the stencil to the underside of the silk.

The two methods just described (direct painting on the silk and tracing paper) are used for large window banners and posters not requiring sharp edges and in fairly short runs (10 to 30 prints).

Sharp edges are hard to achieve with direct painting on the silk if a line runs diagonally to the warp of the silk. This can be understood better if one imagines an enlarged section of the silk. Since the pores in the silk are essentially square and the ink will fill the entire opening, a line running diagonally to the warp will actually be a series of tiny right angles.

A technical disadvantage of the tracing paper stencil is that the centers of letters like O, A, and D will drop out of the stencil. They must be positioned separately under the silk. Of course, after the first stroke of the squeegee the centers will remain in their proper place.

Still another disadvantage of the tracing paper stencil is the tendency of ink to leak under the edge of the stencil. Temporary repairs can be made with masking tape and cleaning solution, but this disadvantage is the main reason that the tracing paper stencil must be limited to short runs.

"Tusche and Glue" is another silk screen technique. The design is made directly on the silk with liquid tusche (crayon dissolved in turpentine). After the tusche has dried the remaining openings in the silk are closed with liquid glue. The glue is poured into the screen and pulled across the silk with a cardboard so that the excess is removed. When the glue has dried, the tusche is washed out with a soft rag and cleaning solvent. The glue, being water soluble, remains as the stencil. This method is especially good for atmospheric effect and copy where a hard edge is not essential.

The most widely used commercial silk screen technique is lacquer film. These films are sold under a variety of trade names. Some are amber and others are green. They all consist of two layers, the lacquer and a backing sheet. The stencil is cut in the lacquer film with a razor-sharp knife. These can be purchased in art supply stores or they can be made to order. Some of the most expensive stencil knives have swivel points so the knife will follow intricate curves.

It requires some practice to cut lacquer film skillfully. The trick is to cut through far enough to strip away the lacquer without going through the backing sheet. Mechanical aids such as protractors, compasses, and French curves are used to achieve neat work.

The completed stencil is positioned under the silk. The back side of the silk is carefully swabbed with adhering solvent on a soft rag. Ordinary lacquer thinner is sometimes used for this purpose but commercially prepared solutions will do a better job because they are designed to match specific lacquer films. It is important that the baseboard exert an even upward pressure on the film during this process. The trick of adhering the stencil, which can be learned best by actual practice, is to use enough solvent to insure good adhesion to the silk but not so much as to destroy the stencil.

When the lacquer stencil is thoroughly dry, the backing sheet is carefully peeled away, leaving the stencil ready for use. After the run, the lacquer stencil is removed with solvent. The lacquer film method permits long runs, gives hard edges, and permits very close color registration.

Silk screen inks are available in both water soluble and oil base. While most stencil films are basically lacquer, there are some water soluble films. Care must be shown not to mix inks and stencils so as to dissolve the stencil.

Color register is not difficult. A master card is prepared. The transparent lacquer films are positioned over the master card. A separate stencil is made for each color. A vertical and horizontal cross hairline is usually drawn on the master card and this is cut in each stencil.

Guides made from folded cardboard are positioned on the baseboard. The master copy is carefully positioned under the hinged screen in the cardboard guides. Each stencil is adhered to the screen with the master copy in this position. It is possible to use one screen for all of the colors in a multi-color design or a separate screen can be used for each color. The only absolute requirement is that the register guides are carefully prepared and that each stencil is adhered after careful alignment on the master.

More than one color can be printed without removing the stencil from the silk by "masking out." The parts of the stencil that are not to be printed are covered with tissue paper or masking tape or filled with a special masking solution.

Silk screen inks in undiluted form are opaque. They can be mixed with transparent base to render them more transparent. Overprinting transparent colors on another gives an interesting effect.

Photo stencils have been developed for silk screen printing that give the effect of a large mesh half-tone. Most silk screen work is a hand operation but machine driven presses are used successfully in volume operations.

Silk screen has several advantages for display work, as compared with other printing methods. "Make-ready" is much easier. Only a small initial investment is required. A frame, a piece of silk, a baseboard, a squeegee, a few inks, and you're in business.

Silk screen inks have an extremely wide range of hue and intensity. The best use of the medium is probably for the production of flat, brilliantly colored designs. Designs requiring greater detail are usually better suited for letterpress or lithography.

Fig. 57

Fig. 58

Fig. 14

Fig. 59

Fig. 60

Fig. 61

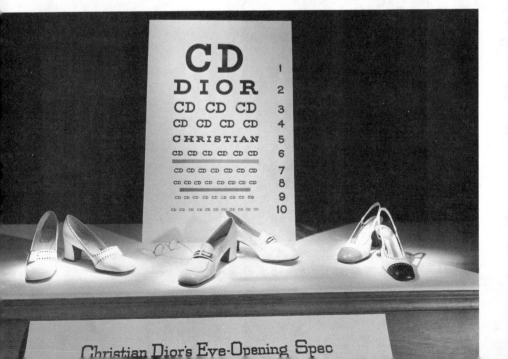

Christian Dior's Eye-Opening Spec

SIGN MACHINES

Sign machines in general display use fall into two categories. These are the punchboard principle and the proof press principle.

The punchboard type consists of a bed, a type case mounted on rollers to permit movement both laterally and in depth over the face of the work, a handle and punch to force the type downward onto the cardboard, and rollers to keep the type inked.

In the punchboard type the letters are printed one at a time. It is, generally speaking, a faster method for one or two copies. If more than two copies are required, the proof-press type machine is faster.

The proof-press type consists of a bed, type that is set on bars or held on the bed by magnetic action, and a roller that is as wide as the bed and moves back and forth along its entire length. The print is made by placing the card stock face down on the inked type and pulling the roller across the back of the stock. The ink is applied with a separate brayer in some cases and with an automatic inking plate in the case of other machines.

As stated before, the proof-press type is faster for more than two copies. They do not possess quite the versatility of the punch-board types. Size of the stock is limited to the bed. Cloth, plastic, and other materials are more difficult to print with the proof-press machines. Various weight stock can be handled by either type. This is done by building up the bed on the proof-press types and by adjusting the downward force of the punch on the punch-board types. It is possible for the operator to do various jobs without constantly washing her hands if she has a punch-board machine. This is especially important in most display departments where one person must double in more than one job.

The quality of the print is about the same for both types. The initial cost is usually a little higher for punch-board types. Secondhand machines are sometimes good investments because, with proper care, machines of either principle are virtually indestructible.

One of the best sign machines, although it is not always thought of as such, is a typewriter. Typewriters can be purchased with display type faces, in addition to the commonly used Pica and Elite type faces. They are very good for making price tickets, selling-point markers, and small signs.

Selling-point markers placed in a neat, uniform manner indicate invisible advantages of the merchandise. For example, the horsepower of a lawnmower, the weight or content of a fabric, the number of jewels in a watch, are all selling points that might well be written out.

Two other machines that deserve brief mention are Multilith and blueprint copiers. These are beyond the budget of most small stores but have found increasing acceptance for sign work in department stores and chain operations.

HAND LETTERING

If the small shop owner or beginning displayman cannot layout signs and letter well it is probably best to rely on machine-made signs or the skill of more experienced persons. Hardly anything ruins an otherwise good display as much as a crude sign. This does not mean that everyone in display should not learn at least the rudiments of this basic skill. The following rules, if practiced diligently, will enable almost anyone to acquire sufficient skill to make acceptable hand-lettered cards.

1. Learn a basic one-stroke alphabet. For practical sign making purposes there are four kinds of lettering; Block Letters, also called Egyptian or Gothic; Thick and Thin, which is based on Roman alphabets; Script, which is similar to modern handwriting; and Text. The last group is called Old English, German Text, Black Text, etc., according to variations on the basic style. Our eyes are not accustomed to the text letter. Because it is hard to read it is limited to use in formal announcements, Christmas displays, and the like.

Mastery of a block alphabet is basic. The displayman should practice with show card paint, a No. 8 or No. 12 red sable show card brush, and newsprint until he has learned to execute this alphabet with precise, assured strokes. Later he can go to more complicated alphabets. The type on newsprint serves as guide lines. A piece of scrap show-card board is tacked to the board and used to work the paint in the brush to the proper consistency. Professional sign painters will testify that much of the success in good show-card work depends on keeping a sharp, chisel-shaped brush.

2. Letter form is dictated by the tool. Ancient Assyrian alphabets look as they do because they were made by pressing wedges into wet clay. Greek letters were square and even because a stylus was the writing instrument. Serifs (the cross stroke at top or bottom of a letter) on Roman letters were the finishing touches in cutting letters in stone. The modern day displayman will letter best if he does not resist the character of the letter formed by the brush, the speedball pen, or whatever tool he employs.

3. Space letters by the "Bag of Sand" rule. Particularly vexing to the beginner is the problem of spacing. If he can think of the spaces between letters as possessing volume and the problem of spacing as

filling the volumes with equal quantities of sand he will get his spacing right.

Letters with perpendicular sides like N or H must have more space than curved letters like O or diagonal letters like A if equal quantities of "sand" are to be "poured" between them. Along similar lines, A and V, or L and T should overlap slightly in order to achieve equal volume between letters.

What about the small shop owner who can't letter and whose budget won't allow a sign machine or the services of a professional show card writer? A good solution is to purchase a set of cut-out letters (they're available in many sizes and styles) for his backgrounds and large signs. His office typewriter can be used for price tickets and selling-point markers.

Cut-out letter sets are manufactured in cardboard, cork, plaster, plastic, Styrofoam, and wood. They can be attached by pins set in the back, by magnetic action, by specially designed adhesives (depending on the manufacturer), and, of course, they can be permanently attached with glue. They can be re-used many times. They can be painted to match seasonal colors. Too many styles should be avoided. The selection of one or two letter styles makes letter replacement easier, also.

In somewhat the same general category are pressure sensitive letters. These are attached to plastic backing sheets and can be transferred to almost any surface by rubbing on the back. These are more commonly used for preparing original art work for reproduction. They can be used for displays if re-use is not an important factor.

SIGN LAYOUT

Sign layout is the arrangement of copy. The headings, the descriptive copy, the price, and any illustrations are the copy elements. Each element should be thought of as a design block. The blocks are arranged on the sign in the most visually satisfying way.

The same principles of balance apply to sign layout that apply to display composition in general. For example, the heading or most important element in the sign (this might be the price or the illustration) is usually not at the exact center of the card. Instead, it is at the optical center or eye level. This is almost always slightly above the exact center.

Sign layout differs from display composition in one important respect. You will recall in our discussion of balance (Chapter 5), we said that the beginning displayman will do well to use a bi-symmetrical arrangement whenever he is unsure of himself. In respect to sign layout, it is generally easier to arrange the heading and descriptive copy on the left margin.

The arrangement of copy so that each line extends equally in either direction from the center requires careful measurement of each line. A legible sign is achieved with much less calculation by setting all copy on the left margin.

STOCK FOR CARDS

Six-ply white cardboard, coated on two sides, is a good display sign board. Railroad board is the name of an inexpensive board that comes in many colors as well as white. Heavier poster weights may be necessary for signs subjected to intense window heat and for extra large readers.

Sign holders are made in standard sizes. Cardboard is cut to match the holders. A so-called full sheet is 22 by 28 inches. 14 by 22 and 11 by 14 inch boards are called half and quarter sheets, respectively, and are used for window readers and feature displays. 7 by 11, $5\frac{1}{2}$ by 7, and $3\frac{1}{2}$ by $5\frac{1}{2}$ inch cards are used for merchandise description. By using standardized sizes the customers are presented with neat, uniform, and easy-to-read signs, while waste (both of cardboard and man hours) is held to a minimum.

CARD TOPPERS

These are signs to supplement the regular merchandise card. Card toppers are added to the regular card by insertion in the top of the fixture. Generally speaking, the same copy is repeated on a number of card toppers. They are used to announce special events, feature buys, advertised values, etc.

Dollar Days and End-of-Month Cleanup are good events for card topper use. The copy should be brief and the color scheme bright and eye-catching. Silk screen is a good medium for their production.

Card toppers must be policed carefully. Thy are meant to be used for limited periods; a weekend, one week, etc. When the event is over they should be taken down promptly.

chapter 9

budgets and paperwork

BUDGETING for display need not be a source of exasperation. It should be defined as *systematic spending to bring maximum return on every dollar spent*. The displayman who chafes under the restrictions of a budget is possibly not aware of the real function of every department in the retail establishment, which is to create sales. The Display Manager who enters willingly into budget planning will usually receive more money than one who has nothing to offer but complaints about past treatment.

It is also true that display has usually been "low man on the totem pole" when the budget is planned. Gradually progressive managers are learning that such an important department needs a larger budget as compared with other promotional media if it is to do its job well.

It is not uncommon to find that newspaper advertising space for a typical department store costs 3 per cent or higher of sales. In stores that spend approximately this percentage for newspaper advertising it would be very unlikely to find a display budget in excess of 1 per cent of sales.

Of course, it can be pointed out that newspaper lineage rates simply cost more than artificial flowers, but this is not the point. The real question budget planners should ask is "How will we get the most return for dollars invested?" If this question is sincerely posed and objectively answered, the display department will wind up with a larger slice of the budget pie.

There are two ways to measure display expenditures. One is a percentage of sales. For example, a store with a sales volume of one million dollars per year and a .075 per cent of sales display budget would spend $7,500. The other is a percentage of store expenses. If, for example, the total store operating expense is $300,000 in the year in question, display would amount to 2.5 per cent of store expenses. Both percentages should be recorded in any display budget.

A recent study by the National Association of Display Industries showed that in a typical New York department store wages run 53.4 per cent of store expense; 15 per cent goes for advertising; shipping and delivery takes 6.6 per cent; and display is at 2.7 per cent.

Perhaps a better idea of what these percentages mean can be had if one understands that the one million dollar volume store used in the example above would possibly have one full-time display staff member. Salaries alone would take at least $6500 of the budget, leaving only $1000 for all other expenditures.

After the percentage of sales that is to be spent on display has been estimated, each section of the budget should be broken down by periods, either weeks or months, dependent on each store's situation.

This estimate must be dependent on past experience. In general the holiday season, or the months of October, November and December, take a much larger chunk of the budget than the other seasons. This follows the rate of sales. In some lines (toys for example) a major part of the total volume is done in these months although attempts have been made to straighten out their sales curves and to secure a more even flow of business. Animated displays, heavier column trims, exterior displays, and more lavish use of foilage in every area is typical of holiday display.

In breaking down the budget into periods it is wise to allow for some flexibility. Although the display budget as set up prior to the opening of the season is the considered judgment of the Display Manager and Store Manager, circumstances frequently arise, as the season progresses, that call for a reasonable degree of flexibility in its administration.

The number of sections in the budget will depend partly on the size of the store. In larger stores a separate section may be kept for each merchandising division, one for windows, and so on. Smaller stores may want to simply divide the total store display expense by calendar quarters. This covers routine expenses such as salaries, window and interior props, sundries, supplies, etc.

This provides an amount that can be ordered in each period. Once that amount has been ordered, no more orders can be written. A record should be submitted regularly by the Display Manager to the Store Manager. This should show the budget for the current period, the amount spent to date in the current period, and the dates of all orders. If the spent-to-date figure exceeds the budgeted figure at any time, ordering must stop. If this or a similar system is followed, the display department will live within its budget.

As was indicated in the section on mannequins, major display expenditures are amortized over a period of years. Mannequins, sign machines, power tools, and basic display fixtures are examples of items that may be included in this group. A separate record should be kept of these items, showing the date of purchase, the date of amortization, and the relationship of this expense to the overall display budget.

A fourth record is kept for determining the overall performance of the sales promotion departments of the store. This is the cost of all publicity and includes newspaper advertising, display, and any other publicity media that are used such as direct mail, radio, TV, or billboards. Total costs for publicity will range from 3 per cent of sales in the case of some discount houses to 5 per cent of sales in the case of department stores and specialty shops.

The salaries of display or advertising staff are included in any percentages that have been given as examples. Not included are capital expenditures, such as remodeling, painting, new carpets, etc. Incidentally, it is imperative for every displayman to know exactly what is being charged to his budget. In some cases what at first appears to be over-expenditure may be a matter of poor accounting. For example, one store charged the samples used for a made-to-measure drapery service to display rather than to the home furnishings department where it belongs. The Display Manager, not being particularly interested in bookkeeping, struggled along for years without the things this money could have provided for his department.

Store managers, like most of us, are most impressed by facts. Nonetheless, there can be no doubt that a little applied psychology should be recalled at budget planning time. A Display Manager should *never* walk into a budget meeting without a plan for the use of the money he will request. This does not mean (in fact should not mean) that he must have the plan outlined in such detail that management can veto the manner of execution or what might be called the aesthetics of the plan. The Store Manager must trust the professional capacity of the Display Manager enough to know that he will come forth with displays that project the desired store image.

The point of intelligent applied psychology is to avoid a negative approach to the money request. Never say "I want more this year because I only got such and such last year" or "I want this figure because advertising gets three times as much" or similar phrases. Instead say "I believe that this display plan (costing a specific number of dollars) can be expected to bring approximately this increase in sales" or similar positive statements.

Also, in connection with the applied psychology of budget requests, many Display Managers will ask for more than they really plan to get and then cut out items they don't really need with a great show of privation. This is a dubious stratagem because the Store Manager will very likely become aware of it and automatically discount what he thinks the budget has been padded.

It is still the practice in most downtown department stores to charge each department whose merchandise is being shown in the windows a daily rental fee based on the space occupied by the goods. This charge, in addition to covering the cost of occupying the window, also helps cover the costs of display salaries, display materials, and lights. The determination of the value of window occupancy and what part this will be of the overall display budget is largely arbitrary.

Many store executives argue effectively against this system. As a result, it has been abandoned in many cases, particularly modern suburban stores where measurement of display space is more difficult because it is more varied and usually interior space. The argument against the system is that it tends to force display into a mechanical routine without regard for the display department's real role as the projectionist of the store's point-of-view . . . of its (poor overworked word) *image*.

OTHER SOURCES FOR DISPLAY FUNDS

A resourceful display department can augment its regular budget. What are some of the sources of these funds? Old props and foliage can be sold or rented to women's clubs and civic groups. Old mannequins can be rented or sold. Profits collected from toyland rides or from photos of children on Santa's lap can sometimes be turned over to display.

Fig. 62

Fig. 63

Windows on a
limited budget

Displays on a
large budget

Fig. 64

Fig. 65

These devices must be undertaken with caution, however. If the display department lets this type of fund raising get out of hand they will find that they are spending more time sorting props and keeping books than they are spending at their real job.

LIMITED BUDGETS—FIRST THINGS FIRST

Inevitably, even the best financed display departments find that they must sometimes cut corners. What are the areas that can be cut? Most experienced displaymen will give a very different answer to this question than laymen.

They will counsel a distinction between those things that only create atmosphere and those that aid in the proper presentation of the merchandise. Good mannequins, proper signing equipment, and basic fixtures, including a modern lighting system would be the absolute necessities. Cutting, if it must be done, can be done with foliage, fancy papers, set decorative pieces, and seasonal materials.

This is not to say that both types of display material do not have a place in your budget. Too many displaymen get the cart before the horse and their work suffers accordingly. Fortunately, a wide range of adequate mannequins, basic fixtures, signing equipment, and light fixtures are available at a wide range of prices within the reach of every store.

FORMS FOR GETTING THE JOB DONE

1. *Sign Requisition:* This is possibly the most used form in any display department. It is used by almost every person in a supervisory position. Merchandise cards, window readers, and special signs are ordered on this form. It should contain the following elements:

   a. Date

   b. Department making request

   c. Size of sign (the choice of standardized sizes will usually be shown on the form)

   d. Space for copy and price (instructions must be included in this section covering the number of letters that can be used on each line and advice on copy writing)

   e. Date required and space for the department manager's initial

2. *Display Requisition:* This form is used by department managers to request in-store displays. Window displays are usually scheduled at promotional planning meetings without the use of this form. Its function is to alert the display department to departmental promotions beyond the ability of sales persons. It should include the following elements:

a. Date
b. Department making request
c. Merchandise and price
d. Nature of the display
e. Area (a number designation if a display chart is used)
f. Date required and space for the department manager's initial

3. *Merchandise Requisition:* This form is given to department managers by the display department. It lists the merchandise needed for any display handled by the display department with pertinent information about the promotion, the turn-in date, etc. A good practice is to attach a blank sign requisition to this form for the department manager to use for reader copy. It should include the following elements:

a. Date
b. Date display will be installed
c. Quantity
d. Size
e. Merchandise
f. Price
g. Special instructions and space for initial

4. *Display Diary:* Develop a system for evaluating a display. This is the only way you can know if the promotion is worth repeating the following year.

One suggestion is to start a Display Diary. An entry in the diary would include the date the display was installed, the date it was removed, a description of the merchandise, the nature of the promotion (style, price, color, etc.), the number of pieces sold while the window was in place, and other comments relative to customer reaction.

Text and illustrations courtesy—L. A. Darling Company, Bronson, Mich.

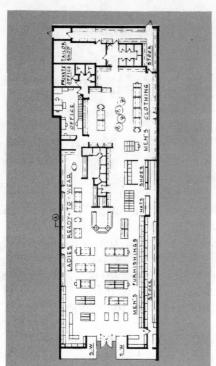

Courtesy—Teichin & Campanella Architects, New York City.

chapter 10

store planning and fixturing

NO DISPLAYMAN who wants to advance into the executive ranks of his store in the future will have much opportunity to do so without at least a fundamental knowledge of store planning and layout, fixturing and the basic fundamentals of visual merchandising beyond those normally associated in the past with window and interior displays.

This chapter will serve to provide at least these fundamentals upon which you can build with experience. There is no substitute for experience in this area. No one can be expected to select fixtures, plan their placement within a store and perform the other store planning and layout functions without having previous retailing experience or having studied the subject seriously under someone with that experience.

Suppose we approach the subject at its most elemental definition stage and proceed from there:

What is Store Planning?

A store plan or fixture layout is a graphic rendition of arrangements of properly selected fixtures to organize merchandise for an effective selling presentation.

Today's complex and competitive marketing of goods requires sound planning from the location, size and type of store. . . . The building . . . parking area to the fixtures and merchandise as well as many other well planned factors.

The merchant's first emphasis is on the merchandise to be sold, from these goods he makes his profit to assist in paying for his basic investment in land, building, fixtures, etc.

It is reasonable to assume if the merchant's first concern is to move merchandise at a profit then he must have adequate equipment to present his merchandise in the most advantageous manner. This equipment being the foundation of merchandise presentation is as important as a foundation of the building which houses his establishment. The engineers and architects who planned the building are considered to be professional consultants and specialists in their field. Their plans are vital and most often are legally required for the construction of the building.

If sound planning is required for the structure then equal or more effort by qualified professional personnel should be employed to obtain a sound profit and foundation through store layout or planning to secure the ultimate in merchandise presentation. Too few people today have the qualifications essential to legitimately advise or properly plan the fixture layout of a store.

Being able to draw does not necessarily make a person a store planner. Almost anyone with some training can draft a legible drawing which is not the most important part of store planning although it is a vital visual record of the results of a formulation of ideas. This is not meant to imply that the actual drawing or the draftsman is not important but rather to emphasize that regardless how impressive and professional the drawing may appear if the end result is not functional then the draftsman has wasted his efforts or talents.

The most important requirement for sound logical suggestions for effective merchandise presentation through proper fixturing is a knowledge of merchandising itself. One must know or acquire a reservoir of sound merchandising principles with the emphasis on the desired exposure by arrangement of the merchandise to be displayed. The merchandise is foremost, the fixture is merely a means for holding the goods to be sold in the best way possible for the most effective method of merchandise presentation.

How does one acquire a reservoir of sound merchandising principles that apply to basic fixturing?

(a) Personal application of all phases of drafting, selecting, installing fixtures and placing of merchandise in proper arrangements including binning, signing and point of sale displays.

(b) Observation. Make a thorough study of merchandise methods of the major promotional and fashion stores. Survey their latest stores shortly after initial openings.

(c) Review and Research. There are many magazines and periodicals directed toward most every known type of stores. As this literature is generally concentrated on merchandise in many phases . . . photographs, sketches and articles can be found to form a file of informative data for future use.

(d) Special or post graduate courses offered by colleges and universities. Seminars by recognized groups of merchant organizations.

To illustrate in simple form the relative importance of the merchandise to the fixture to be selected and to logically accumulate some basic information required to choose the correct fixture and its components, let's use the following list as a guide.

(a) What is the merchandise to be displayed on the fixture?

(b) The quantity of stock to be shown. (How much area on each fixture level, deck, counter tops, shelf or rack is to be allotted for each category of merchandise to be exposed?)

(c) What type of fixture lends itself best for the proper presentation of the specific merchandise to be displayed, to stimulate buyer attention and contain the proper arrangements and stocking accommodations.

Bargain Table	Gondola
Platform	Rack
Counter	Wall Area
Showcase	Others

(d) What size shelves (if shelves are to be used) are required to hold the merchandise itself, its assortment, package or container, garment fold? Size, pattern or color arrangement?

(e) What changes might occur due to seasonal or promotional alterations? Can the unit or a section be rearranged to meet the change?

Many leading retail establishments such as Sears Roebuck & Co., Montgomery Ward & Co. and J. C. Penney Co. employ large staffs of personnel specializing in various categories of merchandising or store planning. Groups of qualified personnel are constantly working with merchandise, arranging and rearranging to find the best visual exposure for each piece of goods to be displayed. Others design the fixture concept. Others specialize in fixture layout, traffic flow, color coordination and decor.

They also employ store engineers and architects on a full time basis to create their final analysis of an ideal functional merchandising establishment. Thorough studies are made by others as to the volume dollar return from each square foot of store area. Each item must have the proper exposure relative to its size, assortment, turnover and dollar return for allotted space.

Naturally in the beginning we cannot match wits or the expenditure of this highly specialized group of experts but we can observe the results of their efforts. Each new store is an open text book of the latest techniques in merchandise presentation. Each piece of merchandise is treated as if it were the only item in the store with consideration given to the possible distracting influence of the vast assortments competing with that item for the purchaser's dollar.

Observe the type of fixture selected for each specific group. Do they use platforms, gondolas, counters, showcases, racks, etc.? Observe the height, width, size shelves and other pertinent elements. One may say, "This is fine for their type of stores and their type of customers but not for us." This might be true to a degree, for instance, their assortments may be larger or smaller, they may not require the same area or aisle space and other obvious circumstances which require variation. The fact is that their customers are well educated by observation to the use of effective presentation of organized merchandising that makes it easier for the customer to see, select, and buy. Why not make use of this tried and proved method of obtaining the full dollar potential from each square foot of selling space which can offer today's retailer the greatest possible return from his display and merchandise investment?

TRAFFIC FLOW

One must know how to capitalize to the fullest on all available selling space of the floor area to obtain the greatest possible return of his fixture and merchandise investment.

Fig. 66:

Floor Merchandisers

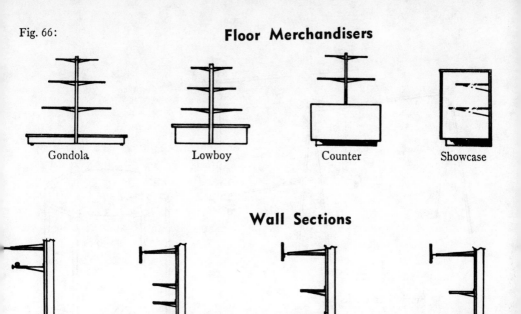

Gondola   Lowboy   Counter   Showcase

Wall Sections

With Hangrails   With Base   With Lowboy   With Counter

Typical Variety of Floor and Rack Merchandisers

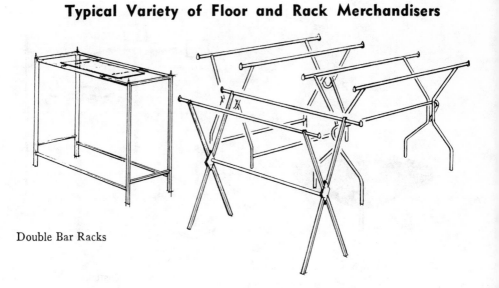

Double Bar Racks

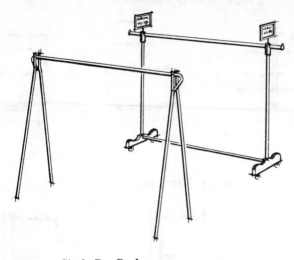

Single Bar Racks

Circular Racks

Skirt Racks

Pant Rack

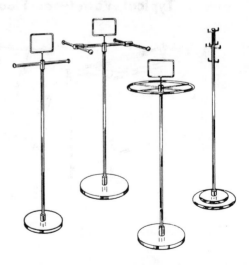

Costumers

(a) Select the proper fixture to effectively present the merchandise to be exposed with the least distracting elements.

(b) The proper aisle space or size.

(c) Traffic floor pattern control.

(d) Best locations of departments and each category of goods within the department to obtain the maximum in sales turnover.

(e) Create a store image by coordinated color, decor, department identification by signs and selecting the fixtures to blend harmoniously to obtain a sales provoking atmosphere to boost sales dramatically.

DECOR

Coordinated color combinations applied to all exposed surfaces requiring finishing are important to the proper merchandise presentation and store image. Paint, wall coverings of paper, vinyl or fabrics, or natural wood grains should be selected to properly frame and enhance the value of the merchandise in its vicinity. Correctly selected decor can be one of the most vital visual aids to atmosphere selling which can boost volume sales dramatically with the least cost of any other item in store fixturing. It *costs no more* to apply the *correct color combination* than it does to use *poorly selected group of colors.*

Pleasant shopping surroundings do have a physiological influence on the customers. Through the proper selection of color, lighting, dramatic but subtle decor effects, one can extend the stay of the customers and gain more sales through prolonged exposure.

POINT-OF-SALE DISPLAYS

Small groups of merchandise elevated above assortment arrangements by the use of stands, forms, mannequins or special display units attract attention to that specific assortment of merchandise.

Today's mass merchandising or full assortment presentation requires spot attention arrestors to intermittently display items in full view. This not only attracts visual observation of the merchandise displayed but acts as a department or section identification symbol.

Too often the merchant forgets or is not interested . . . in the beginning . . . in purchasing these valuable sales aids. He must be reminded and advised as to the importance of point-of-sale displays with traffic stopping impact that act as silent salesmen—continually. Surveys have proved that merchandise individually elevated and well displayed will sell five (5) times faster than goods exposed in the normal manner. An over abundance of elevated displays could have a distracting influence on the customers and could defeat the purpose for which it was intended. Therefore, caution should be taken to the careful selection and location of each individual unit.

The qualified displayman can advise and assist in the selection, quantity and position of each spot or elevated display. Your assistance and knowledge of the equipment available, its function and purpose and its overall effect on store image will be a valuable aid to your merchant-employer.

WHAT DO FIXTURES COST?

This is a logical and ever prevalent question asked by merchants. And displaymen should be prepared to answer knowledgeably. Most times it is asked before the merchant receives a plan or layout, "How much do fixtures cost per square foot?" Of course, this is a question asked by a merchant who really needs assistance because if he is concerned about the best possible sales volume per square foot he would have asked, "How much merchandise exposure can the correct fixtures give per dollar fixture expenditure?"

To further illustrate the comparison of fixture cost on a per square foot basis to sound merchandising, one can use inexpensive, poorly constructed bargain type tables with limited merchandise exposure and figure a per square foot cost much lower than for a more efficient presentation with sound, well constructed fixtures. Prices will vary as to the store image desired in relation to the fixture construction and appearance. A well designed, efficient fixture that gives maximum exposure of goods in a well organized manner to bring the fullest sales turnover is a low cost fixture compared to an inefficient fixture offered for price purposes only.

For a graphic example let's examine the descriptive sketches.

If a merchant purchases his fixtures for price and not function he would possibly end up with units like

(a) With limited Merchandise exposure area.

Let's look at

(b) 40% better

(c) 90%

(d) Over 120% more merchandise area than (a).

If the merchant purchases fixtures (a) for $2.50 a square foot as compared to (c) for $3.10 he will have paid 40% less than what the functional fixtures would have cost that would display 80% more goods . . . or (d) and (e) with 120% increase. This is not the whole story for the most important factor is that it will require twice the

Fig. 67

Merchandise Exposure Area

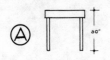

A. 12.5 square feet Merchandising Area.

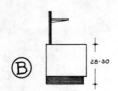

B. Add a 14″ shelf, increase merchandising area over 40%.

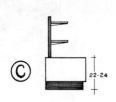

C. Add two 14″ shelves and increase merchandising area over 80%.

D. Add one each 12″, 16″, and 20″ shelves and increase merchandising area over 120%.

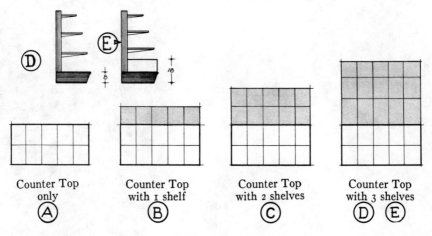

Counter Top only Ⓐ   Counter Top with 1 shelf Ⓑ   Counter Top with 2 shelves Ⓒ   Counter Top with 3 shelves Ⓓ Ⓔ

Fig. 68

Fig. 69

Judy's sporting life

amount of fixtures of (a) to carry the goods as displayed on (c). This raises the square foot price from $2.50 a square foot to $5.00 which is 38% higher than fixture (c). Not only is this false economy regarding fixture cost but it is a waste of valuable floor area and limits percentage of sales on an actual square foot basis.

What is real economy in store fixturing? A fixture that permits the display of the maximum exposure of goods—in the proper arrangement—for each category or line—with the least distracting elements will gain more sales. Thus by amortizing the original fixture cost by the sales gain of the merchandise on this functional fixture . . . one can have real economy in store fixturing.

REQUISITES FOR A STORE PLANNER

Let's for a moment review some of the requisites necessary for a store planner.

a. Merchandising   c. Traffic flow
b. Proper fixturing   d. Relative department locations
e. Point-of-sale displays

Additional requirements should include a knowledge of color coordination, interior decoration, art work, signing and general decor to create the desired store image.

How does one go about selecting the correct colors? This ability, skill or talent is not acquired in a short period of time. Special training can be obtained at various Art or Interior Decoration Schools. This is a longer range plan. A shorter method can be accomplished by the use of color combination brochures or card files supplied by various paint manufacturers. In many cases they supply several complete ranges of colors properly keyed to use together.

Fashion trends in decorators colors change from time to time. For example strong colors were once used and were the fashion during a period, then came the muted tones, pastels, medium tones, etc. Today's soft lively tones of a pastel nature seem to be the accepted concept of the proper colors.

If for some reason one's interior decoration abilities at the beginning are limited, specialists are available as advisors and suppliers of effects through the use of color, wall coverings of papers, vinyl, fabrics and natural wood grains. Others can supply decor pieces, art work and departmental signing.

However, the displayman of today and tomorrow should be able to handle or advise as to correct correlated effect of all phases of this vital atmosphere concept.

If one has or can acquire the fundamental understanding of all phases of store fixture layout and store planning he should be able to authoritatively advise persons seeking these services. He then has the gratifying position of being not only a displayman but can act as a visual merchandising consultant.

As a bonafide visual merchandising consultant one does not necessarily have to do the actual drafting of the plan but he must have sufficient knowledge of and be able to read and have charge of the origination of the graphic presentation of the formulated plan.

Once one has acquired the basic fundamentals of merchandise presentation his assistance becomes invaluable aid to merchants who couldn't possibly afford the necessary expenditure of the merchandising experts of the large chain operations. The smaller merchants require the same up-to-date methods of merchandise presentation to be competitive. This you can give them by offering a professional presentation of effective selling arrangements that can create bigger volume sales and turnover by attracting buyer attention to more merchandise organized in a desired area requirement.

In today's marketing complex more and more goods of different varieties are being offered to a growing consumer market. Distribution of the product is a merchandising problem. New methods of display, packaging, and condensing of exposure areas to accommodate and display these goods requires a fixture of a flexible nature that can adjust to the changing space demands without a major expenditure.

A visual merchandising consultant must not look at just today's problems but must introduce projected visionary requirements for the future. He should be aware that in the future merchandise arrangements will change due to seasonal and special promotions, introduction of new items and rearrangements for various economic and physical reasons.

There is no hard and fast rule or method for a continuing standard for the fixturing of merchandise. Common sense and experience can supplement guess work and errors. Good sound merchandising statistics are the result of good judgment.

A progressive merchant can change or increase the buying habits of the customers in a given area by proper merchandise presentation. He can obtain more of the customers' dollars and procure greater sales volume by attracting buyer attention to more merchandise to stimulate self-selection and impulse buying through applicable fixturing. You as a displayman-visual merchandising consultant can guide the merchant in selecting the best qualified fixture to obtain the desired sales results.

chapter 11

opportunities for displaymen

IN AN informal survey of 30 display managers it was found that 28 [7] listed on-the-job experience as the largest single source of knowledge for their profession. Whether this was an organized apprenticeship or merely knowledge picked up in the course of working as a helper was not indicated. Only eight said they had ever attended specific display courses. This figure would seem to indicate that the trade and art schools, the junior colleges, and the high schools have left an important activity in our modern industrial society virtually untouched.

In this group of 30 display managers, 11 had attended at least 2 years in a university, 12 listed art schools as their main education, and 7 listed high schools. Advertising, art, architecture, engineering, law, and pre-medics were listed as major subjects (with art named the most often) with those who had attended universities.

In the course of their careers it was found that the 30 had worked in an average of 2.8 display jobs. Fourteen of the 30 claimed hobbies that could be called one of the arts, such as painting, photography, home decorating, music, and so on.

APTITUDE

What does all this indicate? It appears that displaymen value practical experience very highly. While they are largely art-oriented, they are an extremely diverse group, coming from almost every background.

A liberal arts education is perhaps the best general background for display work. The specifics of the craft can be learned on the job if necessary. A graduate of a professional art school may be more prone to boredom with the business aspects of his work. The liberal arts graduate, with a broad sampling of the arts, literature, the social sciences, and language arts is most apt to bring the necessary largeness of viewpoint to his display job. These are admittedly broad generalizations. No doubt many exceptions can be cited.

Can we generalize further and say that certain aptitudes insure a successful display career? Certainly an aptitude for visual perception is absolutely necessary. The ability to recognize balance, rhythm, and unity in a display is part of the day-to-day routine. This ability can be partially acquired but there can be little doubt that some persons have this aptitude in greater degrees than others.

An equally important but sometimes ignored aptitude is business ability. Contrary to popular belief, an artist is apt to be quite unhappy in display work if his interest is only in design rather than in sales.

STANDARDS AND COMPENSATION

Department stores have three job categories, generally speaking, in their display departments. These are apprentices, helpers, and journeymen. Journeymen rates at the time of this writing, while not as high as the building trades or certain mechanical crafts, for example, are not an exact picture of prevailing standards.

Most employers pay premium rates to displaymen with outstanding ability. This is true even in departments organized by unions. Union contracts, contrary to popular belief, only set the minimum rate and do not prohibit employers from paying premium rates if they so desire.

The rates paid to apprentices are based on a periodic increase that will bring the apprentice to journeyman rate and the title within a specified period. Examinations and practical work tests can be a part of the arrangement.

Of course, the jobs that most displaymen in large corporations aspire to are those of assistant display manager or display manager, or even higher executive positions. These can be quite lucrative, especially if the company has some kind of a management incentive plan. While it is perhaps true that in the past most top executive jobs in the retail structure have been filled from the merchandising departments, there is increasing evidence that the sales promotion departments are assuming an ever larger role.

FREE-LANCE DISPLAY WORK

Specialty shops and companies serving the public outside of the retail field (banks and savings and loan companies, for example) often employ free-lance displaymen. This can be a very rewarding field.

A special temperament is required to succeed in free-lance work. The most common failing is to underprice. A realistic view of the time and materials that go into the job must be made clear before the job is undertaken.

A contract is advisable with free-lance accounts. This does not have to be elaborate. A written document, setting forth the terms of the job, and signed by both parties, will prevent many misunderstandings. The contract can specify an hourly rate that will cover all materials as well as the displayman's time, it can be an hourly rate plus an amount for materials, or it can be a flat rate for the job, with the frequency of change, etc., written out as part of the contract.

DISPLAY CLUBS AND ASSOCIATIONS

Many major cities have display clubs. Membership is open to any person in the display field. The clubs hold clinics on display techniques, they promote higher standards and recognition for display, in an informal way they post their members about employment opportunities, and they organize city-wide promotions. This last area of activity is a tremendous opportunity for alert displaymen.

There is an organization called the National Association of Display Industries. It organizes market weeks, usually in New York City, for the purpose of previewing the offerings of display manufacturers for the coming season. In addition, NADI conducts surveys and distributes material of general interest to the display profession.

TRAINING

An increasing number of schools are introducing display courses. The retail industry has told them that even in a period of technological unemployment, qualified displaymen cannot be obtained in sufficient quantity.

Possibly the greatest weakness of the display courses that are offered is a failure to emphasize the practical, day-to-day requirements of the work. In short, the craft of display building is minimized.

Teachers are borrowed from the business or art departments. The physical facilities for practicing display techniques are very limited. The "cart is usually put before the horse," that is to say a "theme" is developed and the merchandise made to fit the theme.

Good display courses must make merchandise paramount (perhaps by closer coordination with retail establishments). They must be practical. There is little value in allowing a student one semester to develop his "theme" and to trim one "model" window if he will be expected to execute several such displays every week when he leaves school. Of course, he must be "allowed to walk before he is made to run" but he must not be trained to believe that "walking" will always be the norm.

MAKING OPPORTUNITIES

Opportunity is in every display department. It is in the rapidly unfolding evolution that not only affects retailing but every facet of our lives. The display manager who will prosper is the person who does not leave the growth of his store to chance. He will make every effort to understand the changes that are emerging. He will develop new ideas accordingly for the growth of his store. Innovations may be in self-service methods, they may be in store planning, they may be in new display materials, they may be in lighting, or they may be in areas that we cannot even comprehend at present.

The significant thing is to experiment, to study, and to use new ideas forcefully and imaginatively. The display manager who knows how to make his opportunities will not let display stand still. He will build on the sound traditions of the past a new and exciting display world for tomorrow.

glossary of familiar display terms

Apprentice
A beginner in display work, usually holding a contract of some sort with his employer, setting forth the terms and length of his training.

Asymmetrical
Division of the display space into unequal parts.

Backlight
Atmospheric lighting behind the display area, usually projected from the floor with fluorescent tubes.

Bank
Windows, tables, or other display areas in sequence, in which several compositional elements are repeated.

Bi-symmetrical
Division of the display space into equal parts.

Boarding
The use of corrugated or other cardboards as pinning surfaces to give merchandise a neat, crisp look.

Buyer

A store employee who buys at wholesale one or more lines of merchandise. Buying involves much more than the placement of orders. Constant study of current trends in his lines, merchandising, and promotional planning are all important facets of the buyer's job.

Card Topper

A sign to supplement the regular merchandise card. Card toppers are added to the merchandise card by insertion in the top of the fixture. Generally speaking, the same copy is repeated on a number of card toppers. They are used to announce special events, feature buys, etc. They should only be used for clearly specified periods of time.

Chroma

The intensity or saturation of a hue.

Comparative Price

Two prices, announced simultaneously, the first being the former higher price, the second being the present lower price.

Dealer Display

A display piece, usually complete within itself, offered free or at minimal cost by a manufacturer or wholesale dealer. Also called point-of-purchase displays.

Divider

A screen, panel, or other fixture for separating windows. Dividers are usually removable.

Drop-in

A small display inserted within the compositional framework of a larger unit.

End or Cap

A table or other fixture at the end of a stock-keeping fixture. Located on peak traffic aisles, end or cap areas are prime display space.

End Use

The way an item will be worn, used, hung, driven, etc., after it leaves the store. End use display involves showing the item in a setting made to look as natural as possible.

E.O.M.

End-Of-Month Cleanup, a traditional promotion in many stores.

Eye Level

That point in a window or other display area that is a horizontal extension of the line of sight of a person shopping.

Flat

A board of varying dimensions, usually constructed from wall-board and light lumber for the construction of display backgrounds.

Font

A printer's term used to designate a set of type all in the same style. Sign machine type and cardboard cut-out letters used in display work are also called fonts.

Frame of Reference

The perpendicular and horizontal edges, either real or implied, of any display space.

Gondola

A large, two sided, multi-shelf fixture for the stocking of merchandise.

Half Sheet
Half of a standard 22 by 28 inch show-card board or 14 by 22 inches. A quarter sheet is 11 by 14 inches.

Hard Line
Furniture, appliances, machinery, and similar hard merchandise. The opposite of Soft Line which is clothing, bedding and linens, etc.

Hard Sell
A popular expression in the retail industry signifying a sales message of maximum persuasive power.

Heavy
Large amount of merchandise; synonymous with stocky or full.

Helper
A member of the display department staff. In many cases the starting pay for a helper is more than for an apprentice but they do not have as much chance for advancement.

Hue
One of the three attributes of color. The name of common usage; yellow, orange, red, violet, blue, green, and so on.

Impulse Item
Merchandise that is apt to be purchased by spontaneous inclination because of its inherent character. The opposite of staple or planned purchase.

Institutional
A display designed to set forth an aspect of policy, history, tradition, etc.

Island
A display area that can be viewed from four sides.

Journeyman
One of three basic groups of display workers. Journeymen are considered skilled, having completed a period of apprenticeship.

Key Copy
Four or five words on a sign that summarize the meaning of a display. Often the boldest lettering.

Light
A small amount of merchandise.

Line
A stock of merchandise of various qualities and values in the same general class.

Loss Leader
Merchandise offered for sale at cost or below cost to attract customers.

Lower Case
Print in small letters. The opposite of capitals.

Merchandise Card
Show cards of uniform dimensions ranging from 3½ by 5½ inches to 14 by 22 inches setting forth the description and price of adjacent merchandise. Designed to fit metal holders. Sometimes called "silent salesmen."

Nippers (dikes)
A small tool. The correct name is diagonal cutters. Invaluable to displaymen.

Open Display
Merchandise arrangements in which customers can pick-up and inspect before purchasing.

Perimeter
The outer boundary of a store interior. Often this is wasted space that can be utilized by an ingenious person.

Perspective
The arrangement of objects in display to give the illusion of procession in depth.

Point-of-Purchase (also Point-of-Sale)
The place where the merchandise selection is actually made. Slightly misleading because the point-of-purchase and selection point are not the same in self-service stores. Good point-of-purchase display can create phenomenal sales gains. See Dealer Display.

Prop
Short for property. The various adjuncts of a display except the merchandise and fixtures.

Pull (2 meanings)
A display that has the power to attract customers is said to pull; also to disassemble a display.

Reader
The principal card or sign in a display. So-called because it is sometimes phrased in conventional form.

Related Item
Merchandise that is related in terms of function; slippers with sleepwear, neckties with shirts, beach towels with swimwear, and so on.

Rig
A term used in men's wear display to indicate the process of dressing mannequins and forms.

Rotation
The systematic change of displays to maintain a fresh appearance in the store.

Scatter
Shredded plastic, wood, paper, or cork used to simulate grass, stones, or to make abstract shapes on the display floor.

Seamless or No-Seam
Paper in rolls ranging in size from 2-inch ribbon up to 107 inches by 50 feet. In many colors, relatively inexpensive, seamless is widely used for display backgrounds.

Set-Up
The arrangement of mannequins, fixtures, and devices for achieving height. The display background is usually considered a separate element in composition.

Sig (logo)
The name of the store in a distinctive design that is repeated in all promotional material. Sigs of important brands are also used in display.

Special Event
Holidays, traditional sales periods, and local promotions, around which the promotional plan is built.

Stylist
A member of the display staff, specially trained in the selection of accessories and all matters pertaining to the lady shopper's taste.

Traffic
  The movement of shoppers in and around the store. Traffic jams are encouraged by displaymen.

T-Stand
  A basic fixture, consisting of a base, an extensible standard, and a horizontal bar. In various sizes, T-stands accommodate many merchandise lines. Other tops can be substituted for specialized displays.

Unit
  A coordinated grouping of merchandise. One of the principal elements in display composition, the others being the background, the set-up, the accessories, and the reader and price tickets.

Upper Case
  Capital letters. The opposite of lower case.

Value
  The range of grays from black to white.

Wash
  An indirect light; as opposed to spotlighting.

acknowledgments

Fig. 1: Telchin & Campanella Architects, New York City.

Fig. 2: Retail Reporting Bureau, New York City.

Fig. 3: Telchin & Campanella Architects, New York City.

Fig. 4: Telchin & Campanella Architects, New York City.

Fig. 5: John Wanamaker, Philadelphia.

Fig. 6: Lord & Taylor, New York City. William MacElree, display director.

Fig. 7: Neiman-Marcus, Fort Worth, Texas. James Hale, display director.

Fig. 8: Neiman-Marcus, Fort Worth, Texas. James Hale, display director.

Fig. 9: The Author.

Fig. 10: Walker-Scott Co., Escondido Village, Escondido, Calif. Designed by Brand-Worth Associates, Los Angeles. Photo by Rutledge.

Fig. 11: Maas Brothers, Tampa, Fla., Kai Frost, director visual merchandising.

Fig. 12: Franklin Simon, New York City. Jess Sweeney, display director.

Fig. 13: Philips' Lighting.

Fig. 15: Bergdorf Goodman, New York City, John Quinn, display director.

Fig. 16: General Electric Company.

Fig. 17: Russell Shaw, Orlando, Fla.

Fig. 18: Russell Shaw, Orlando, Fla.

Fig. 19: Russell Shaw, Orlando, Fla.

Fig. 20: Best & Co., New York City. Robert Benzio, display director.

Fig. 21: Abercrombie & Fitch, New York City. William Withers, display director.

Fig. 22: Bergdorf Goodman, New York City. John Quinn, display director.

Fig. 23: Henri Bendel, New York City. Billy Giblin, display director.

Fig. 25: Bergdorf Goodman, New York City. John Quinn, display director.

Fig. 26: Frederick & Nelson, Washington, D. C. George K. Payne, display director.

Fig. 27: The Author.

Fig. 28: The Author.

Fig. 29: Macy's, Jamaica, New York. Liam Bromley, display director.

Fig. 30: Macy's, Jamaica, New York. Liam Bromley, display director.

Fig. 31: Mark Cross, New York City. Ron Prybycien, display director.

Fig. 32: Lord & Taylor, New York City. William MacElree, display director.

Fig. 33: The Author.

Fig. 34: Hollywood Vasserette, New York City.

Fig. 35: Belk of Columbia, Columbia, S. C. Buran Jarrett, display director.

Fig. 36: Bergdorf Goodman, New York City. John Quinn, display director.

Fig. 37: Lord & Taylor, New York City. William MacElree, display director.

Fig. 38: Ohrbach's, New York City. Ed Mitchell, display director.

Fig. 39: Marc Cross, New York City. Ron Prybycien, display director.

Fig. 40: Belk of Columbia, Columbia, S. C. Buran Jarrett, display director.

Fig. 41: The Author.

Fig. 42: The Author.

Fig. 43: Gump's, San Francisco, Calif. Robert Mahoney, display director.

Fig. 44: Marc Cross, New York City. Ron Prybycien, display director.

Fig. 45: Paul Stuart, New York City. Salvatore Cesanani, display director.

Fig. 46: Magasin Du Nord, Copenhagen, Denmark. Bent T. Kilaa, display director.

Fig. 47: Castletons, Salt Lake City, Utah. Richard Conrad, display director.

Fig. 48: Franklin Simon, New York City. Jess Sweeney, display director.

Fig. 49: Belk-Hudson Co., Spartanburg, S. C. Chino Tyus, display director.

Fig. 50: Bergdorf Goodman, New York City. John Quinn, display director.

Fig. 51: Magasin Du Nord, Copenhagen, Denmark. Bent T. Kilaa, display director.

Fig. 52: J. E. Caldwell Co., Philadelphia, Pa. Frank D. Root, display director.

Fig. 53: Woodward & Lothrop, Washington, D. C. George K. Payne, display director.

Fig. 54: T. Eaton Co., Winnipeg, Canada. Janice Baumann, display manager.

Fig. 55: Vaughn Parades, Inc., Miami, Fla. Frank Cloutier, designer.

Fig. 56: American Standard exhibit, New York City.

Fig. 57: Henri Bendel, New York City. Billy Giblin, display director.

Fig. 58: Toledo Edison Co., Toledo, Ohio. Owen Mauk, display director.

Fig. 59: TWA, New York City.

Fig. 60: Bergdorf Goodman, New York City. John Quinn, display director.

Fig. 61: Delmans, New York City. Howard Nevelow, display director.

Fig. 62: Belk of Columbia, Columbia, S. C. Buran Jarrett, display director.

Fig. 63: B. Altman, New York City. Raymond Gent, display director.

Fig. 64: Saks Fifth Avenue, New York City. Henry Callahan, display director.

Fig. 65: Saks Fifth Avenue, New York City. Henry Callahan, display director.

Fig. 66: Courtesy of L. A. Darling Co., Bronson, Mich.

Fig. 67: Courtesy of L. A. Darling Co., Bronson, Mich.

Fig. 68: Brown Shoe Co., Robert M. Woodruff, store planning division.

Fig. 69: Judy's, Los Angeles.

Esta edición ha sido preparada por
Ediciones del Castillo, S. A.
Marqués de Monteagudo, 16. Madrid-28
Depósito legal: M. 2.963-1976
Impreso en Artes Gráficas EMA
Miguel Yuste, 31. Madrid-17